Kelly Pres

Kelly Preston: Unscripted

"In Hollywood circles, Kelly is known as "The Iceberg."

As they say, most of the iceberg floats dangerously under the surface."

Robert Randolph

Kelly Preston: Unscripted

Kelly Preston: Unscripted

John Travolta's

Hopelessly Devoted

Wife

EXPOSED!

Robert

Randolph

Once upon a time,

Long before Kelly Smith became Mrs. John Travolta, she found herself at the local movie theater where she and a friend watched Grease, starring John Travolta.

While watching the movie, Kelly informed her friend that someday she was going to marry the movie star.

And so the scripted story began – 1991

Presenting: *Kelly Preston, Unscripted* – 2015

Robert Randolph

Kelly Preston: Unscripted

Kelly Preston: Unscripted

Contents

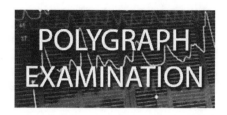

I think of myself as a new breed of writer, where my books are completely based on the truth – I back that truth up with a polygraph examination in the beginning of all my books.

I feel the truth is much more important than perfect grammar or experience with writing books. I have found that most people, if given the chance, *can* handle the truth, and if given a choice, they would prefer it. For many years now, we have all been reading the edited, cut down, celebrity-approved version of the truth when it relates to their lives.

I am proud to be a new breed of truth tellers that will bring you the truth at all costs. Or at least, I can start my book with a lie detector test to try and show you this is a place where you are going to be reading the truth, not fiction. I challenged anyone to prove me to be a liar with my first book *"You'll Never Spa in This Town Again"*, in particular, John Travolta. He never took

3

me up on that challenge and he never sued me for defamation of character, or for any other reason.

I make the same challenge to Travolta or Preston, or anyone else who may want to question whether this book is fact or fiction.

Sincerely,

Robert Randolph

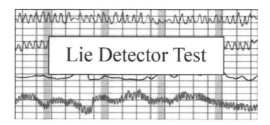

1.   Were you contacted by family members and employees of Preston's?

YES

2.   Were you completely honest about everything you wrote about in this book?

YES

3.   Were you shown a picture of Preston one month before the birth of baby Ben, while in a swim suit where she appears *not* pregnant?

YES

4.   Where you contacted by several women claiming to have been lovers of Preston's and long term girlfriends?

YES

5.   Did you see several pictures of actress, Kirstie Alley and Preston in sexual embraces with each other?

                                                            YES

6.   Did you get an email from a prostitute claiming to be Charlie Sheen's girlfriend where she said Sheen wanted to talk?

                                                            YES

7.   Were you given permission from all your sources to publish their stories in this book?

                                                            YES

8.   Did you personally meet every source and ex-employee who contacted you?

                                                            YES

9.   Did you receive extremely incriminating documents regarding Preston and her now mysteriously missing first child?

                                                            YES

10. Were you shown text messages between Kirstie Alley and Preston making plans to have an evening of sex with S & M overtones to it?

YES

11. Did Mark Riccardi, John Travolta's exclusive stunt double in fourteen films, expose many of Preston's addictions and sexual perversions he had personally witnessed while working for Travolta?

YES

12. Did you see a copy of what you were told is the fake marriage agreement between Travolta and Preston?

YES

13. Have you received multiple death threats regarding the release of your books relating to John Travolta and Kelly Preston?

YES

14. Is every detail that you have shared, regarding Kelly Preston and her *unscripted* life, to the best of your knowledge, 100% true and accurate?

YES

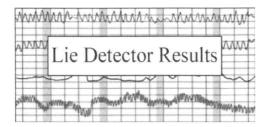

Conclusion:

"After carefully reviewing the polygraph charts of the subject (Robert Randolph), it is the opinion of this examiner, that there was no indication of deception during the polygraph examination."

-From the report of the polygraph examiner I worked with on April 26, 2015

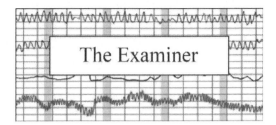

The Examiner

When the time came for me to get my polygraph test done for the book, I was very selective of whom I wanted to do the exam. I knew I wanted someone with an extensive background in the field, and that is exactly who I found. He is one of the top polygraph examiners in the world.

He was once a U.S. Secret Service special agent. He also worked the Protective Service Detail for the white house and remained there long enough to have four different presidents as his superior. He has over sixteen thousand polygraph examinations under his belt and has testified in both state and federal courts. He is trusted by state and federal public defenders' offices to perform polygraph tests and he is called on often to review the polygraph examinations conducted by law enforcement agencies to see if there were carried out properly. This is a mere partial list of the accomplishments he has achieved during his long and highly revered career to say the least.

Dedication

This book is dedicated to all my sources who have helped to make this endeavor a reality. Thank you for taking the time to reach out to me and encourage my journey for the truth regarding the Travoltas. It has been a wonderful experience to undertake. You know who you are, your stories are included.

There are others whose *positions* have prevented me from officially acknowledging their assistance, however, their unstinting contributions have been invaluable.

These individuals have put their jobs, careers, and in some cases, even their lives in jeopardy, while taking the risk to bring the facts to the public's awareness.

Please know . . . your efforts did not fall on deaf ears . . . this book is dedicated to you!

Opening Statement

In writing this book, my intentions are to expose a side of Kelly Preston the public never has the opportunity to see . . . the *unscripted* side! I will show how nearly every facet of Preston's life is discussed and directed through the principal handlers of The Church of Scientology and how it has been that way since she was first recruited into the *fake* marriage.

It is believed that Travolta will see her dead before he would allow her to ever leave his side or the Church he uses to imprison her. Before each and every interview, Preston is drilled relentlessly, for hours, to ensure that she gets the story straight. When she makes a mistake, she is punished in a way equivalent to the retribution normally reserved for the greatest dissidents within the CoS.

Is it any wonder that Preston has turned into an alcoholic, pill-popping, distraught woman? From the very start, every little detail about Preston has come to us hand-crafted by Travolta and the CoS – leaving her nowhere to run.

Preston, unlike Katie Holmes and Leah Remini, has not yet made it out alive; she is still living a life she misguidedly chose nearly twenty-five years ago. Never will Preston be given the option of getting a divorce, nor the experience of truly loving a man and living a transparent, truthful life for all the world to see. It would appear that this is, in all likelihood, Preston's final act.

Leah Remini was the best thing to happen to Preston from within the CoS; not only was she Preston's *only* insider friend, Leah was more like a mother figure to Preston's daughter, Ella. Leah helped make up for the love and affection Kelly and John could not, and would not, give to their children.

Take everything about Preston you know and set it aside for a moment; give yourself a chance to read the unscripted truth about one of today's greatest actresses. That's correct, I said *greatest* actress. I believe that by the time you're finished reading this book, you will agree, that in order for Preston to be able to pull off so many deceptions and lies, she could only be one of the greatest actresses out there! *Scripted* is what we have on record regarding Kelly Preston. It is my hope to bring you, through this book, a better understanding of the woman through truthful, *unscripted* tales. Tales only an authentic insider could bring you! The stories were all so over the top, there is no way I would ever think of publishing this book without beginning with my customary polygraph test, just as I did with all my previous books on Travolta.

Author's Notes

Many people would consider John Travolta to be a great actor, at one time, and as the saying goes, "Behind every great man there is a woman." The type of woman he has had by his side for the past twenty-four years may help to explain his lewd and insidious behavior. I have already chronicled said behavior in a series of books depicting his escapades in public spas. I believe this woman enabled and encouraged Travolta to become the sexual predator he is, acting out his sexual addiction, almost daily.

I asked myself for several years, could I write the truth regarding what I had learned about John Travolta and Kelly Preston's marriage? Could I reveal to the world that their marriage is, in fact, a sham; their entire life together, as seen by the public was fake? Could I do it? After much consideration, the answer was "yes." While doing research for the Travolta books, I was blindsided by so many people, including: previous employees, new and former assistants, ex-lovers, family members, friends, hair dressers, and party boys/girls, all contacting me with their stories about Preston! It was really something of a treasure chest of secrets.

To say I was intrigued with Preston's secrets and sex life would be an understatement; I found it exciting to know she was not sitting at home knitting mittens for a man who will never really be *her* man. In reality, Preston had a secret life of her own. Well, not all her own, because if that were true, I wouldn't have so many sources. It was reported to me that Preston has been known to put people "in the ground," with a look of her eye aimed at her Scientology handlers. The secrets I am revealing will shock you into a heightened sense of awareness and you will feel assured that you are reading the truth.

I spent many restless nights contemplating how to bring these stories of Kelly Preston, along with all her special friends, to light. In what style should it be written? How was I to ensure that it would be easy to follow the web of secrecy that was about to unfold?

It came to me . . . just tell it as it happened! To the point, true, and basically unedited. I have always found that to be the best approach and as difficult as the truth can sometimes be, it has always served me well. My life has been many things, but never boring! I was amazed with all the insider stories told to me by some very kind and interesting people.

The best part, by far, since writing my books on the truth about Travolta, has been hearing from so many of his fans, as well as Preston's fans, who have reached out to me and asked that I tell my story. I was blown away with who my sources were, from all walks of life. I was thrilled! To learn there is so much interest in the woman, who is the focus of this book, was an eye opener. I knew that since these people had turned to me for help, just as the victims of her husband did, I would speak out for them as well. It seems somewhat amusing how, just when I think I'm getting away from Travolta territory, they keep pulling me back!

My early impression of Preston was very naive and, as it turns out, completely wrong. Like most of the public, I originally tended to believe her and Travolta's *scripted* life as portrayed in the media. But after learning her real story, which includes household secrets from the bedroom, to the garage, to the backyard, I soon realized that girl was on fire! The uncovered lies and real stories revealed to me, over and over by those who had firsthand knowledge, was more than I could have imagined. Preston really did have her own secret life going on as well and here I was, sharing in this information.

An observation which I found interesting — out of all the correspondence I received, of which there were hundreds, none ever said anything of a positive nature regarding either Travolta or Preston. Another bond the two apparently share, is their commitment to their arranged marriage, intended to fool their fans — and the world.

Decide for yourself . . . did she settle? It is a question you can only answer after reading what I have to expose.

Introduction

I would like to say I came away from writing this book with a fondness for Kelly Preston, but that is hardly the case. The deceptions I uncovered about the *scripted* life that she, along with famous husband John Travolta, has been living and selling to the public for decades, left me disgusted! I resolved myself to the task of bringing out the truth, saying to myself, "It may be a dirty job – cleaning up all the bullshit the Travolta's are putting out to the world – but someone's got to do it and it may as well be me!"

When word first got out that I had a book, revealing John Travolta's secret sex life, in progress and soon to be released, titled *You'll Never Spa in This Town Again*, I began hearing from men all over the world who had sleazy stories to share regarding JT's sexual antics. Along the way, I would also receive many fascinating emails on the subject of Preston and her own lurid adventures while her hubby, Johnny, was busy having sex at local spas with just about everyone in sight. As long as people trust me with their accounts of JT and Preston, I will be here to share those stories, as well as my own, with the public.

Right after my first *National Enquirer*, world exclusive story broke in September 2010, many men began seeking me out for advice and help regarding scandalous claims of sexual abuse they had experienced at the hands of JT. Some may have simply needed a sounding board to listen to horror stories of their sexual encounters with Travolta. Whatever their objectives, I felt I was the unofficial, one man, human resource department charged with helping the victims of Travolta's sexual assaults.

Early on, I believed Preston was an innocent victim, deceived by her philandering husband as much as the general public was. But after extensive research, I can now assure you, nothing could be further from the truth. The facts which have surfaced about the woman, are sure to make the hair on the back of your neck stand on end. An innocent victim? Hardly.

From the time of Kelly Preston's birth (a.k.a. Kelly Kamalelehua Smith), on October 13, 1962, her life has been overshadowed with ambiguities and suspicions, which carry as much intrigue of some of the greatest mysteries of our time. From her ever changing birth name to her disappearing first child, from her 1985-1988 marriage to actor and convicted felon, Kevin Gage.

She had stars in her eyes and was given the world, but what do you do when there is no one to share it with? In Preston's case, she turned to booze and pills, drinking away the torment of a marriage to one of the world's most acclaimed and closeted homosexual movie stars. I was informed, repeatedly, that Preston actually thought she could turn John straight. After years of futile attempts at making their marriage something real, Preston finally realized that it was a marriage in name only.

Is it any wonder that Preston would fall back into old habits of drug and alcohol abuse? I have known a few women in my life who desired to change my sexual orientation but I was always honest with them. At times, I had very fulfilling heterosexual relationships, so I know it is possible to be with the one you love, enjoy the moment and not define it within a sexuality category.

It soon became apparent that I was sitting on a potentially fabulous book on the subject of Preston, who is among the most obvious beards in recent memory. Using beards to support the deception of Hollywood's leading homosexual male celebrities has a long history. A few examples are: Cary Grant had Barbara Harris; Rock Hudson with Phyllis Gates;

David Geffen had Cher; Elton John with Renate Blauel, and the list goes on for days.

What was originally planned as a chapter in one of my books about her husband, ultimately developed into a palpable book dedicated to many of the things that make Kelly Preston tick. Not only were average Joes contacting me regarding the Travolta's, but celebrities were reaching out to me and sharing their own experiences and knowledge as well. I had the opportunity to meet with interesting friends of Preston, in addition to several of her family members, some of whom were disappointed with the life she has chosen to lead. Many were tremendously forthcoming with their details of her *unscripted* life; I found the particulars enthralling. I believe you will too!

Imagine, if you can, the absolute delight I felt the day I opened an email from one of Preston's high profile, ex-lover's current girlfriends. Right smack in the middle of his very public meltdown, according to his girlfriend at the time, this well-known actor was eager to discuss Preston, in order to set the record straight, regarding a story in which he had "covered for her" decades earlier. Preston's ex was partying with a "winning" spirit and sounded extremely intoxicated when we did eventually speak over the phone.

The time would come for me to share my thoughts on this fascinating and complicated woman; I believe that time is now. There are so many interesting stories to tell. From the bogus pregnancy of her child, Ben, to the mistreatment of her now deceased son, Jett – I will challenge Preston to counter my claims and put them to rest. Can she produce pictures of herself while pregnant? How about producing physical proof offsetting the evidence I have seen which verified she was, once again, doing damage control over the death of her son, Jett (by faking her pregnancy). All the while, struggling to get the *Travolta* name back out there as being synonymous with a heterosexual family image.

I will touch on the subject of Jett Travolta in this book; his full story is coming soon, *The John Travolta & Kelly Preston Autism Cover Up: The Tragic Life and Death of Jett Travolta*. Every person on this planet deserves to be accounted for, including a movie star's son who did not live up to the star's, or his church's beliefs and expectations. Jett wasn't even gone a few months when they announced the upcoming birth of another child.

At the time of Jett Travolta's fatal seizure, he had been left by himself, unattended in a marble constructed bathroom. Meanwhile, Preston was upstairs, in the arms of her celebrity lover, liquored up and nearly comatose. She had not seen Jett for over thirteen hours. How tragic is that? Imagine you had a dog you knew had seizures, would you leave that dog alone for thirteen hours unattended? I didn't think so.

This woman had the opportunity to change the world with the truth of her son's autism but, instead she elected to lie by telling us it was Kawasaki Disease. Only on the witness stand, under oath, did John Travolta *finally* admit his son, Jett, did in fact, have autism. That was 2011, so for all of Jett's sixteen years, Travolta and Preston lied to the entire world.

Christina Crawford was able to set the record straight in her book recounting her childhood, and life with her mother, actress Joan Crawford. In *Mommy Dearest*, Christina, shares so much of what she endured being raised by the movie star. Young, innocent Jett had *two* crazy movie stars as parents, who follow this century's weirdest, cult-like church's teachings. He was never given the opportunity to tell his story nor allowed to have medication that may have saved his life! Wait until you read what I learned – you will be shocked as well as saddened,

23

but will come away with a true, inside look into one of the most disturbing stories of child neglect and abuse that had been going on in front of the world's eyes.

I found the cold manner in which Preston treats people to be typical alcoholic, pill- popper behavior. Is she living the dream she thought she had bargained for, or sentenced to a life of liquor, wearing the beard label until the day she dies? I found her to be a total fraud, and a Hollywood solution to a movie star's predicament, hence, the marriage. Putting all the undesirable qualities about Preston aside (of which there are many), more than anything, I was left with a feeling of indescribable sorrow for the children who call her "mother." When you learn the facts, you will come away knowing the real Kelly Preston.

I will close with a final thought for you to consider . . . It is often said that, "Behind every great man is a great woman."

I would add to that by saying, "Behind every closeted gay celebrity is a beard."

Welcome to *Kelly Preston, Unscripted.*

"I was a complete mess until Scientology came into my life. It

has taken me countless years of auditing and studies to

achieve what I have become within Scientology. I owe the

Church my life and sanity."

Kelly Preston (2000)

Scientology

Although I covered this topic in my book, *You'll Never Spa in This Town Again,* the Church of Scientology (CoS) plays such a major role in the lives of John Travolta and Kelly Preston, I thought it necessary to revisit the subject here. They are both devoted members of the Church, as are many of their closest friends, so a little background may prove useful when trying to make sense of the events as they unfold.

Many celebrities are attracted to the CoS possibly due to the special attention the Church offers them. They are considered so special that Celebrity Centers have been established in several major cities around the world, for their convenience. According to the Operation Clambake website, famous, rich, and powerful people are important to the cause due to their "great marketing value." Kelly Preston was told about the CoS, by an acting coach, early in her career. Based on what she learned, she believed she could have it all. It was through her connection with the CoS that she first met her future husband, John Travolta.

The CoS website describes their faith as a new religion, founded by *Dianetics* author, L. Ron Hubbard. Its members apply learned principles and knowledge to enable them to achieve the ultimate goal of spiritual enlightenment in their daily lives, as well as freedom for all. It is considered a way of life – not a system of beliefs or faith. Scientology claims to use modern advances in technology to answer age-old questions, such as "Why are we here?" and "Where did we come from?"

Many who have been closely involved with the CoS, including some who were once members, explain how believers are taught that they are "super human," and receive intense training through costly classes. Scientologists are convinced that psychiatry and psychology are corrupt and humans are able to fix themselves, without prescription medication, when it comes to mental illness. Oddly enough, in spite of all the so called, "modern advances in technology," L. Ron Hubbard was unable to cure himself of whatever drove him to commit suicide.

The CoS website explains that humans are, by nature, basically good. "Scientologists actively use the insights and knowledge that Scientology gives them to make a real, positive difference in the lives of others." We can become evil by thinking and acting only for ourselves while not considering how others may be affected. Men and women must work to solve their problems and make their own lives better. By doing so, they put themselves in a position to help others by using their power, ability, and basic decency. Among the CoS fundamental truths are:

- Man is an immortal spiritual being, not just a material object
- His capabilities are unlimited, even if not presently realized
- His experience extends well beyond a single lifetime

In addition to the aforementioned truths, which few would dispute as being a very rational, level-headed way of thinking, it is essential to point out some of the other "truths" the religion also observes:

- Scientologists believe homosexuals are mentally ill and a menace to society
- Scientologists do not accept or tolerate autism or depression. Instead, they find anyone affected with these common ailments as worthless and contaminators of the Earth

- Millions of years ago, an evil alien (XENU) populated the Earth with billions of people, whose souls must be cleansed from modern-day people.

"Auditing" sessions are used within the CoS to improve many distressful conditions by confronting and handling them. It is considered, by the CoS, to be a very precise and exact process of obtaining spiritual awareness and freedom. However, some who have left the CoS, refer to the auditing method as a way to weaken the mind, or "brainwashing." The auditing process does reveal a lot of dirty laundry, sometimes making it impossible to walk away. Nevertheless, there have been celebrities strong enough to sever ties, but have often expressed concerns and fear after doing so.

Even as the CoS continues to grow, so do the number of dissidents, many of whom dread retribution. The CoS has been accused of being more of a "criminal organization." As resourced on the Operation Clambake website, there are those who believe the CoS ". . . is a vicious and dangerous cult that masquerades as a religion. Its purpose is to make money." Scientology is said to be a "banned" subject when it comes to interviewing powerful members. Questions regarding their connection to the CoS are often agreed, beforehand, to be off limits. In the HBO documentary, "Going Clear," the CoS has denied the accusations.

In 1980, Reader's Digest quoted science fiction author, L. Ron Hubbard as saying: "Writing for a penny a word is ridiculous. If you really want to make a million dollars, the best way would be to start his own religion." Boy, he got that right! After all, *The Bible* is, and will probably continue be, the #1 bestselling book of all time. It has been written and rewritten, printed and reprinted, more times, and in more languages, than any other book in history. Why not jump on that wagon?

The Travoltas' are among many big name stars considered to be successful Scientologists. It appears as if the CoS plays a major role in every aspect of their day to day lives, public and private, mundane and scandalous. You name it, and the Church of Scientology is involved.

Our kids are the center of our universe, I'm so different too.

Now I don't smoke anymore.

I don't do drugs anymore. All of those come with an

'anymore.'

I used to do everything and a lot of everything.

With drinking I just decided that I wasn't always at my best.

There were times where I drank too much, for sure.

And when I didn't drink, I felt amazing, and I woke up

feeling amazing every single day."

Kelly Preston (2013)

A First Marriage, a Missing Child

In the midst of all the media attention I was getting from 2010 – 2014, due to the release of my book chronicling John Travolta's massage scandal, there were many lawsuits coming out against Travolta practically on a daily basis, two of which I was personally responsible for, (Fabian Zanzi's and my own). During that period of time, I would end up hearing from a staggering amount of sources concerning all things Travolta and Preston. I was pleasantly surprised to hear from many of Preston's immediate family members. I was even able to verify their authenticity, (see polygraph #3). Several began, for the most part, sending emails encouraging to me to go forward with my stories about Travolta. However, some also stepped up to advise me, the way only a family member could, about the "unscripted" side to Kelly Preston.

Allegedly, there were many nights during Preston's childhood when she would accompany her mother, to her job at the psychiatric ward, and help out when they were short staffed, which, I'm told, was often. One of Preston's cousins told me she had "seen things involving crazy people that would make your head spin!" I understand Preston became very skilled at "giving people the juice with the electros" during the shock treatment. Some even said she seemed to get off on it because she couldn't get enough of "shocking the retards at the nut house."

I was told that when Preston was very young, she had a boyfriend from the ward where her mother worked. The story goes that Preston and this boy were secret lovers. Unbeknownst to Preston, her boyfriend was a straight up lunatic who had been committed for killing his entire family during a manic episode. He shot them all dead. Amazingly, Preston did not know he was crazy; when they told her he was a patient and not an employee, she had what was known as her first mental breakdown. She went off the deep end when she realized she had been in love with a psycho without having a clue he was off balance. She took that whole experience very hard.

Her relatives were eager to share their stories about their famous relative. They were all in agreement on how Preston could not wait to get off the Hawaiian island and move to Los Angeles to become an actress. What no one saw coming, was the marriage to Kevin Gage; after all, Preston was adamant that she would never get married back in those days. They went on to tell me how Preston had a reputation as being the

"Island Slut." She was known to smoke pot all day and screw surfers, tourists and various locals. The marriage took place because Preston and Gage were expecting a baby, and even though she had an extremely lurid reputation, she didn't want the baby to be born "a bastard."

Gage and Preston shared a love for dope, but not so much for each other. Her cousin said, "He grew it and she bought it. Then she realized that if she fucked Gage, she could get her weed for free by using her pussy." Unfortunately, as stated earlier, she would become pregnant very early in their relationship and it would ruin everything. The saddest thing, her relatives pointed out, was that while Preston was pregnant with Gage's child, she drank like a sailor. She even used cocaine up until giving birth, which was one month premature – undoubtedly due to Preston's habitual partying throughout the entire pregnancy. She did come close to losing the baby, but of course, it survived. She knew that because of her life style, the baby was born disabled, which was unacceptable to the actress and her vision of how her life and child *should* be.

While pregnant, Preston was always cheerful while talking about anything relating to the baby. Once the child was born with severe down syndrome, she refused to publicly claim the child as hers anymore. It would be Preston's mother, Linda Carlson, who would take him in under the pretense of the child being just another patient she cared for at the mental institute. Preston knew then that she had to stay away from the mental hospital and could never go back. She would decide years later, once it had soaked in that her child was truly disabled, her mother must hide the child and raise it privately.

The child was named Trent, after Kevin's grandfather's best friend who had saved Kevin's life when he was a little boy. A heavy bird bath had fallen on top of him and was crushing the life out of the child, when the friend came to the rescue just in time. With young Trent in the institute and securely out of the way, Preston felt absolutely no obligation to stay married to Gage. She had already become quite bored with the whole relationship. In fact, she complained about how boring he was on their very first date so now imagine how she must have felt after a few years being married to him. It comes as no surprise that they called it quits and got a divorce.

It would not be until later, when Preston married a high powered Scientologist, that her past transgressions had to disappear – including, but not limited to, Wikipedia pages, websites, and any other derogatory records that could be found online. Her history was all cleaned up through the trusty services of the Church of Scientology. They attempted to get rid of the truth surrounding Preston's shocking previous life. Try as they might, the past always had a way of finding its way back to the internet.

The Travoltas' purchased a home in 1996 on the Hawaiian Island of Oahu; more precisely, it is located at 5797 Kalanianaole HWY, Honolulu. The residence was used as a place to keep Trent hidden from the public eye and it was Linda Carlson who moved in to watch over the boy. Considering Carlson didn't meet her famous son-in-law for nearly fourteen years, this appears to be further evidence that the Travolta's had little or nothing to do with Trent.

The last thing I heard from one of the relatives was that Trent Gage was missing and they were extremely concerned. They were afraid that Preston, or possibly the Church of Scientology, had taken the child in order to destroy him so there would be no chance of the truth ever coming out through DNA testing or otherwise. Especially since there were times when the family members had reached out to Preston to warn her about how she should start taking better care of her disabled son. They threatened to expose the truth and shortly thereafter, coincidentally, Trent was gone. It is highly unlikely that such a severely disable child could have left on his own, so they concluded that he must have been taken by Scientologists, as well as Preston. Thus, for the moment, the child missing from Preston's Wikipedia page is the same child missing from her life. (Information about the child appeared on Preston's original Wikipedia profile, before it was removed. (See pages 205 & 206). I asked all her relatives, point blank, about what they knew regarding Preston's involvement with Trent. They all had a very similar answer, "She will go to hell for the way she has treated that child!"

Since the child had gone missing, there was no longer a need for Linda Carlson to stay in the Honolulu house. According to my sources, Carlson did not take the news well, to say the least. When she was ordered to move from the waterfront compound, she became unglued, swearing to get revenge on both Preston and Travolta. I was told that she had been preparing, for some time, for this situation and would do whatever she had to do to destroy her daughter for ". . . tossing her aside like garbage." My source continued, "They don't know who they're dealing with, but they sure will when she's finished with them!"

Another thing Preston's family told me, which I thought was rather strange, was the fact that they didn't meet Travolta until the two had been married for almost twelve years. During one meeting, "Kelly put on a real show for us all. She was showing off her movie star husband, who kept cruising Kelly's very good looking cousin, right in front of us." In addition, Preston had intentionally stayed away from her mother, whom she truly despises. Some believe that may be because "she blames her mother's polluted genes for causing her to keep throwing out damaged kids."

I walked away from my time with Preston's very candid and honest family feeling blessed to have met them. They trusted me with their anonymity and privacy while letting me know many of the gritty details, so the truth could finally be exposed. They made this a wonderful experience, and I came away from it with hope for Trent Gage and his safe return. I believe if Preston had taken proper care of her first born son, many of her family members would never had contacted me or shared their concern for the child who is now missing and presumed kidnapped by the Church of Scientology.

"My husband, Johnny, and I play dirty stewardess

when we're alone on the plane, and we love to go to cheap

motels for quickies."

Kelly Preston – (2001)

Hoping to convince the world he's straight

The Secret Marriage Contract

It was around 1989 when the Church of Scientology's highest ranking officials began considering Kelly Preston as a proper, submissive wife for their problematic leading member, who seemed to be having difficulty keeping his dick in his pants as well as overtly chasing men all over town. Between 1988 - 1991, Travolta had been in the tabloids for all the wrong reasons. Increased public awareness, regarding his homosexuality, was going to be a deal breaker. That is, unless they could get him married off to another Scientologist of the opposite sex. They theorized that the world was not ready to have their hottest heartthrob, one known as a womanizer and a stud, outed in the tabloids for having sex with male porn stars. Worse yet, the porn stars were consistently quite burly looking. The ultimate conclusion drawn would have to be that Travolta was a submissive bottom, not a dominant top. The answer was . . . Kelly Preston.

Preston had been regularly hanging around the Hollywood Scientology center during this period. She had a reputation as being an attractive woman with not much going on in the way of brains. She was also known for having serious drug and alcohol problems, my source, Anita, explained. It seemed Kelly was the perfect fit – her career barely existed and she would be easy bait for Travolta. It was a win-win situation. Perhaps she thought once she married the big movie star, she would surely be catapulted to the A-list category. However, everyone involved in the CoS must have known they had their work cut out for them pulling off this "marriage." They must have also known that once it was a done deal, Preston would be their *prisoner* forever. They would own her and her every move for the rest of her life. Quite a price to pay!

This was to be Preston's fate. Anita explained how Travolta and Preston met during the filming of "The Experts," and while they had a blast making the movie, there was never the slightest thought of romance between them. This was because, Anita explained, "Kelly thought of John more as a girlfriend – *not* a boyfriend. They shared the thrill of chasing cock together when they weren't on set working." Anita went on to say, "Let's face it, that woman could drink anybody under the table, and once she did, she was likely to fuck them while they were under there."

This was anticipated and posed a problem for the CoS, as their agenda was to convince Preston to sign on for a life with Travolta, not only because they knew he was homosexual, but because they knew she had personally accompanied him on so many of his exploits with other gay men. "It was as if they were just a couple of *girlfriends* who partied together and slept around." Anita added, "Kelly was known as the *fag-hag,* although it was meant affectionately. Most gay men have had a fag-hag friend or two in their lives."

"The plan was to explain to Preston how Travolta needed a lot of work at the center. After he had enough auditing, he would be *cured* and no longer be a queer. He would then want to willingly fulfill his vows as a husband, but only after the Church rid him of his demons."

Anita said that, "It took Kelly, less than one minute to accept the offer. It wasn't even necessary to go into all the perks they were offering. As soon as Kelly heard she was going to be made into a major movie star, with a guaranteed three picture deal, and all she had to do was marry Travolta, she was ready to go get a drink and celebrate." Anita told me how the high ranking Scientologists were elated; they knew they had just hit the jack-pot for Travolta, landing him a submissive wife. Preston would soon undergo a very intense cleansing of her own demons. Once they brainwashed her into becoming the ideal woman, it would all be smooth sailing. Or so they thought!

In addition to the three picture deal, she was promised a beautiful home (in her name), and $500,000 for every year she stayed married to Travolta. They even threw in an additional $50k per child, as a bonus. If a child happened to be born with a defect, it would not be considered Travolta's fault since they already deemed Preston as the person with internally damaged goods. (refer to page 209). Not surprisingly, there were many issues which needed to be resolved before this whole *marriage* thing could be put together. The number one problem was a man named Paul Barresi, who was said to be looking to make a few bucks shopping a sex story around town of himself and Travolta.

Anita said her duties during this time included accompanying Travolta everywhere he went, twenty-four-seven. She was to be his personal assistant in many ways, however, her predominant responsibility was to keep a close eye on his every move and inform the CoS officials of his activities. Whenever Travolta went to a sex club or a bar looking for cock, Anita was there to report on him. Anita described it as a time when, "the Church was going crazy with Travolta getting fucked by just about every man in town, while Preston was drinking guys under the table before fucking them."

Since Anita had been sticking so close to Travolta, she was well aware of how the news of Paul Barresi wanting money to keep quiet, greatly upset Travolta. He became a basket case, urging the Church to finalize the marriage deal with Preston – the sooner the better. As soon as word came down from the high ranking officials within the CoS that the paperwork was completed and ready to go, the two were called to headquarters for signatures. Travolta fully understood all the fabrications they had implanted into Preston, to which he agreed and signed off. What he didn't realize at the time was that, while he was playing a part in selling Preston's soul, he was selling his own as well. Anita summarized how "from that moment on, the Church of Scientology would own John Travolta until he died and then some. After his death, the Church will be getting it all, not the children or the wife, but the Church."

As previously stated, the fear of Barresi's story coming out had Travolta in an absolute catatonic state – he could not function, even though he had a major film coming out. When the studio got wind of Barresi's allegations, it was made clear to Travolta that if the story was believed by the public, he would likely be washed up in Hollywood as a leading man. It was with this warning that both Travolta and Preston sold their souls. He could not wait another minute, even though he already knew the marriage would be a sham. He was in full damage control mode – a role he will likely play for the rest of his life.

So the story could break in time for the upcoming weeks' tabloid deadlines, the two were wed on September 5, 1991. It took meticulous effort to stem the surge of gossip from the National Enquirer story, which had already come out, spilling the dirt about Travolta's affair with Paul Barresi. However, when the public learned how Barresi had passed several polygraph tests, they could now believe the rumors about Travolta *were* true.

Even though they had their pictures posted all around the world as a *happily married couple*, they were not yet legally married. They needed to complete the deed, which they undoubtedly went into, knowing it was a sham from the first moment the marriage of convenience was suggested. The couple would go through a legal ceremony on September 12, 1991, not because they necessarily wanted to, but because it would make the union very legal, and very public. "Signed, sealed, delivered," is the way Anita described her firsthand look of the nuptials and inner workings involved in putting these two horribly flawed people together.

When remembering the time just prior to severing ties with the Church, Anita told me, "One day I was in the office of records, performing my hours of free work, when I came across the contract between Travolta and Preston. It was very simple and to the point. I immediately knew, after I stumbled upon the file cabinet, I had found the ticket to my escape." Anita said she had been looking for her way out from the Church and knew she would need real fire power in order to fight her way free, "So I copied the whole files on John, Kelly, and Tom Cruise."

Anita continued, "My entire family had been working within the Church for years. First as paid servants and then later as, albeit reluctant, members. The CoS made it impossible for my father to say 'no' when they told him he must join and bring his entire family with him. This practically killed my mother because she was a devout Catholic; she wanted nothing to do with this, so called *Church* of Scientology."

"In time, my poor mother gave in to my father's wishes and from that day on, she died a little every day. Eventually my mother did pass away from natural causes, but I will always believe it truly was from forsaken faith and a broken heart."

I was pleased to learn that now another former Scientologist (Anita), was able to find her way free from the CoS. Like Anita, almost all the people who reached out to me, had the same foresight before defecting from the CoS. They all grabbed whatever documents they could get their hands on to use as insurance to break away from what they now perceived as a cult. With proof in hand, they would be able to gain their freedom without intimidation and threats of murder.

"Please don't believe the trash out there. It's just trash.

Absolute rubbish — they couldn't be happier, they're over the moon."

Linda Carlson, Preston's mother — (2012)

(Adding her two cents worth of bullshit to help cover up the fake marriage.)

Linda Carlson: The Mother of All Mothers

Taking into consideration Kelly Preston's many issues, along with her lifelong (self-admitted), addiction to drugs and alcohol, is it any wonder her birth mother, Linda Carlson, would have more than her share of skeletons in the closet? Preston's mother was an administrator at a mental health care facility in Hawaii and is reported to be quite a "nut." Preston's stepfather, Peter Palzis (who also adopted her), married Carlson when Preston was very young but they divorced when she was fourteen. My Palzis family sources had proven to be very revealing. These immediate family members contacted me to say that they had not heard from Preston in over a decade. It is safe to say that there was certainly a great deal of animosity toward their movie star cousin – the one who never gave any of them the time of day.

Many in the immediate family were furious at Preston for turning her back on them for so many years. They held nothing back when it came time to share their stories with me. These internal family sources had no love loss for Preston or her mother, and spared no detail. It was one story after another.

"Kelly was the little Island tramp," one uncle alleged, while her cousin claimed that, "Kelly had tried heroin when she was eleven years old."

Linda Carlson's family generously shared with me the details of what they described as a cold and calculating mother to the troubled actress, a mother they claim Preston truly despises and cannot stand to be around. Carlson was a damaged woman in her own right, with two failed marriages under her belt. However, her marriage to Preston's birth father was never legal and Preston never knew him. Her father is said to have drown when Preston was only three years old. What was not said publicly, was the fact that Linda Carlson was the prime suspect in what was thought to be a murder – not an accidental drowning. She was off the hook when the coroner, ultimately, could not find any evidence of foul play and was eventually forced to rule the drowning an accident. With a big sigh of relief, Carlson moved on with her life, continuing to set the example for Preston on how to screw up her life.

Supposedly, Carlson had her own substance abuse problems – hence, her extended career with the mental hospital. It provided opportunities for her to get drugs, since she practically ran the whole place. Young Kelly Preston saw everything her mother did, including alleged murders of convenience of several elderly patients. Carlson, according to my sources, did much more than just take kickbacks and pilfer drugs. She was suspected, but never charged, of helping some of the patient's relatives to move on with their own lives by getting rid of their aging family members while they were hospitalized.

Back in the 1970's, Carlson became known as one of the toughest women to run a facility for the mentally disturbed. She was also investigated for being the ring-leader of an elder abuse scheme that was conceived for the purpose of separating countless senior citizens from their life savings. The unsuspecting patients were being robbed blind. Thus, when you hear Linda Carlson is a cold, calculating woman, you can see where it stems from.

It comes as no surprise that Preston would become known throughout Hollywood as "ice berg Preston" and "pussy with a purpose Preston." With a mother like Carlson, it could be possible to destroy an innocent child and create a raging monster in her place. In this instance, Carlson did just that, but as far as monsters go, this one had a particularly vicious temper!

Carlson made no bones about her bitterness toward her daughter for waiting so many years to finally bring her big movie-star husband around for their first meeting. After all, she had been playing up her role as *mother in-law* in the media for well over a decade and yet, she still had not met her son-in-law. In addition, no photographs exist of Carlson and Jett together; remarkably, she had never known, nor even met her grandson. According to my source, the entire family agreed that making Carlson wait for nearly fourteen years before introducing her to her son-in-law was not a smart thing to do. As one family member remarked, "Linda holds a grudge like nobody else can and she *will* get even with both Kelly and John."

During Preston's childhood years, heroin had gained popularity on the Island and she would become heavily involved. Her addiction took her from one end of the island to another, in search of *johns* and *tricks* to help finance her dope. Hawaii was quickly becoming one of the busiest places on earth for heroin and Preston wasted no time getting close to the head distributers and dealers. She worked hard to position herself to play an important role among her band of addicts and drug lords. According to her family, Preston was fast becoming one of the Islands biggest attractions during these years – it seemed that everybody wanted to meet her – because she was now the head dealer . . . period!

Preston delighted in the street level notoriety that came with being the top dealer on a little island in the middle of the Pacific. It was during this time that her family would become painfully aware of her use of drugs, as well as her need for the spotlight. This is when she made up her mind to become a star and the rest is history.

There are many different versions of how this story played out. *This* is the way it really went down – as told by her own family. "A need for drugs and guys with fast cars," is how one of her cousins summed it up. Although he had not spoken to her in over eighteen years, the cousin went on to tell me that the main reason Preston left the island is because she was on the run. She was expecting a visit soon from detectives who were investigating her mother, Carlson, in the alleged murder scandal. "She left town and headed for Los Angeles to avoid being questioned." He went on to point out, "I would love to tell you that my cousin and I are close, but we are not. Quite honestly, I don't expect to ever hear from her again."

The way her family described it, Preston . . . "walked away from her family years ago. She only mentions us now because we live in the time of the internet. She knows she can't write us off, at least, not completely." The family source went on to say, "The fact that she uses our family name, yet never bothers to speak to us, is a slap in the face! We all know she is in a pretend marriage intended to fool the world."

Like her mother, Preston's other relatives were equally upset and offended at being excluded from the world of Travolta. She maintains a minimal amount of contact in order to make it appear as if she is on good terms with her family, but that is far from the truth.

I received many negative comments from family members, such as, "My cousin is a cold-hearted bitch!" and, "My Aunt Linda [Kelly's mother] is the one who started it all." I walked away from my time with Preston's family thinking they seemed like decent enough people and that it was a real shame their famous relative didn't even know these people who shared her bloodline. Instead, they behaved more like enemies than family. The dark realities surfacing, came from a dysfunctional family's internal breakdown. Many sources I met while researching this book have had stories they were eager to share, but one thing consistently stood out – the fact that no one ever mentioned Preston having a single redeeming quality. Leaving Hawaii to flee from her troubles only got her so far. Preston would depart Hawaii with several monkeys on her back. Hard-core alcoholic. Pill-popper. Heroin addict. To put it mildly, the woman was a downright wreck.

"She's not worried about it at all.

She's not concerned, my daughter told me she hasn't given it one thought."

Linda Carlson – (2010)

Preston's mother's reply when asked if Kelly was concerned about being pregnant at nearly fifty years old.

The Fake Pregnancy

I was beyond surprised when I was contacted by a woman who had read my book, *You'll Never Spa in This Town Again,* claiming to have known Kelly Preston extremely well for more than twenty-one years. Although this woman had previously defected from Scientology, she carried with her a suitcase of truth containing incriminating memories, invaluable to solving the mystery surrounding Preston, who at the age of forty-seven, fabricated her pregnancy. In lurid detail, my source shared with me the reality behind the lies, intended to fool the world, of an impending birth from within the Travolta marriage. My source described how she had left the CoS and was in deep hiding for her own safety, but wanted to reach out to let me know about the bogus pregnancy.

As it turns out, my source had been Preston's personal handler, and goes by the name of Lu. Lu said she is now living in a state far from Los Angeles and that she would be more than happy to give me all the facts regarding the plan to fool the world with Kelly Preston's pregnancy scam. She went on to explain to me how a pregnancy apparatus was discretely ordered right off the internet – no big Hollywood production needed for this fake baby bump. Lu recalled how after Travolta had sat through hundreds of hours of makeup in order to be transformed into a woman for *Hairspray*, he logically realized that he and Preston could pull off the same effect, in mere minutes, without anybody suspecting and no chance of it being leaked out. My source noted how all parties were sworn to the utmost secrecy.

It had been Lu who received the package that was delivered containing the fake pregnancy supplies. She showed me pictures of the baby bump they bought and I don't mind telling you, it was really creepy. I was looking at a plastic device designed to give the allusion of pregnancy. Knowing that it was used to fool the entire world in a fraud pulled off in the name of Hollywood, gave me goose bumps. (See page 210).

Lu reaffirmed that only a handful of people knew about the scheme Travolta and Preston were about to pull off, in their attempt to get the public off the subject of the wrongful death of their deceased son, Jett. Seemingly, both Travolta and Preston were fearful that, considering the direction main stream media was heading in 2009, after Jett had just died, there was a very real possibility that they would be charged with neglectful treatment of their son. As is now commonly known, Jett was autistic, a fact that Travolta only admitted on the witness stand in 2012. He had been lying to the world for Jett's entire sixteen years of life by claiming Jett had Kawasaki disease. Amid all the lies and cover-ups, there was going to be a real baby. The biological mother of the new baby was to be a young Scientologist from within the Church who was already pregnant.

The plan was to adopt, or *take* this new born baby. Once the scheme was approved by the CoS hierarchy, the wheels were set into motion. Lu showed me several pictures of Preston which were taken right before allegedly giving birth to the child named Ben. Looking at the pictures, it is 100% clear that Preston was not pregnant at all! My jaw dropped as I was shown picture after picture of Preston, in a clearly non-pregnant condition, just days prior to Ben's birth date. There were many comments being made online regarding the fake pregnancy, and it now makes sense. When you look at pictures of Preston during the alleged pregnancy, she appears to have never even gained a pound. When I Googled "Kelly Preston" for pictures after the alleged birth of baby Ben, it was so obvious she had lied about the whole thing. Try as I might, I couldn't find one picture of Preston, anywhere, where it was clear to see she was pregnant. Only in the stomach area did she appear larger.

Lu said one of her jobs was to accompany Preston to all the *outside* functions, meaning events which were away from the CoS. She went on to say that on a couple of occasions, while out at events, the pregnancy apparatus had come undone, and they realized they needed to be more careful. I was astonished that these Scientologist celebrities had succeeded in fooling the entire world of the truth of this child's actual source of origin. In fact, there are pictures on the internet showing Preston, a mere month after the birth, and she looks to be exactly the same weight as a month before the alleged birth. I can't help but wonder why they didn't use more caution to help ensure their lies were not so easily unraveled. After all, anyone familiar with Google could easily come to the same conclusions I have.

Preston could have stayed in hiding for several months after the fake birth, then explained how she was having a tough time losing all the pregnancy weight. But no, not the Travolta's. They would go on to boast, in interviews, that Preston never had such an easy pregnancy and how she was able to lose all the baby weight in only one month! It's always been my understanding that losing weight gets harder and harder with every pregnancy and especially as a woman gets older, but not for Preston!

Lu accompanied Preston to the Cannes film awards a month before she supposedly gave birth to baby Ben and Lu said Preston was actually losing weight due to her heavy drinking. Lu alleged how, right about this time, Preston was really out of control and threatening John that she was going to tell the world all their secrets. According to Lu, Preston was drunk twenty-four hours a day. She went on to explain that as time came closer for the birth, Preston was a total wreck. Though she was a pro at pulling off countless lies and performances in the past, this time she was extremely nervous, scared and unable to stop the booze.

The night of the Cannes film festival, Lu described Preston as being on pills and drunk on vodka. Just before hitting the red carpet, Preston threatened Travolta, over the phone, that she was going to kill herself. Had she attempted her suicide threat, the world would have certainly found out about the sham since she should have been much larger if she really had a baby inside her forty-eight-year-old body.

The game plan was as follows: As soon as the baby was born at the Hollywood Scientology Center, which was set for a predetermined date, Lu was ready to put into action the switch and cover-up. Her job was to dispose of the pregnancy apparatus by burning it. However, when the time came, she said she did not throw it in the downstairs furnace but instead stashed it behind a nearby bin. Lu went back for it a couple of days later and since it was the weekend, there were fewer employees around the center. I asked her why Preston would be at the center at the time of the swap, and she explained that "Everything went down there." Lu went on to clarify how this is how they could deliver the new baby using their own Scientologist doctor, placing the baby in Preston's possession in order to dupe the public.

I questioned, "If the real mother of baby Ben was already pregnant before the Travolta's came up with the scheme, doesn't that mean John is not the father of the baby?"

"Bingo!" exclaimed Lu.

I was already floored with all this news being revealed to me but then to find out that John was not even the real father hit me like a bombshell. Lu added, ". . . the real father was actually a higher up in the Church who had dark features and could pass as a Travolta relative if you squint your eyes."

Lu laughed when I remarked, "So I guess that's what we need to do whenever we look at the child, just squint!"

Lu and I would get together on three additional occasions and at each meeting, she brought the suitcase which was always filled with more incriminating objects for sharing. She said she kept the pregnancy suit which had Preston's DNA on it, along with other items, to guarantee her safety against retaliation from the CoS. When I asked her why she would contact me to share this information, she responded, "Why not?"

"When you're in for life, you're fucked." Lu added, "Kelly is a straight up bitch and gets her jollies from telling her stories and lies. She will do whatever it takes to get the job done. She's in for life."

Lu elaborated by saying she felt reassured with the idea of Preston and Travolta knowing that she had reached out to me with her story; she said to her it served as more protection. "The last thing in the world they want is for all the information I have on them to be made public. The fake pregnancy was only the very tip of the ice berg – I have been keeping secrets, notes and collecting evidence for two decades from within the Church." As it happens, one of the previously mentioned secrets being kept by Lu, is that one of Preston's original lies was with the pregnancy of Jett. I was informed that, although Preston was pregnant with Jett and did, indeed, carry him herself, she had undergone in vitro fertilization to become pregnant. They believed this is how baby Jett developed autism.

As I watched Lu drive away, I speculated what would become of all these Scientologists who were making the decision to reject and leave the Church. I also wondered if I would ever have the opportunity to share this over the top, *fake pregnancy* story with anyone. Here I am feeling thrilled to be doing just that!

I was somewhat aware of Preston's involvement, and obvious participation, in the *scripted* life, which she and Travolta had been presenting to the world for decades. However, I was not fully aware of the lengths she would go to keep her *scripted* life intact. It seems there is nothing on this planet that she would not do, in the name of her career and her individual quest for happiness. To be honest, putting on a pregnancy suit to play the public like a bunch of suckers, pretending to be expecting a baby, exceeded even my suspicious imagination. This was a real eye opener for me, especially after seeing the pictures of her non-pregnant body for myself. (See polygraph question #3) All Preston would need to do in order to dispute this truth, is to produce pictures of herself pregnant but that would be impossible since THEY DO NOT EXIST!

The Academy Award for the greatest performance from a female, in the leading role category of lies, goes to . . . Kelly Preston!

"As a friend, when you know someone you care about is

hurting, you try to do whatever you can to ease their pain and

get their mind off of their troubles."

Kirstie Alley – (2012)

About her friendship with Kelly Preston

Kelly, Kirstie, and the Assistant/Lover

While planning my upcoming book on John Travolta's wife, *"Kelly Preston Unscripted,"* I had no idea that Preston and Kirstie Alley had been hooking up. I had already written a few chapters on Preston when I received an email from a girlfriend of Preston's who was upset about being dumped and was ready to talk. I knew, from my experience with the previous books I wrote on Travolta, that an email like this could potentially be dynamite.

Immediately after reading the email, I replied and asked to meet with her. She was nervous but wanted to talk, so we agreed to meet at Norms on La Cienega in West Hollywood. I got there early and waited inside for her with great anticipation, wondering what type of evidence she would bring. My mind was whirling with so many ideas.

Never, in my wildest dreams, could I have imagined what was about to be revealed. Through the years, I had heard, from many sources that Kirstie Alley was a Lesbian and, by her own admission, hadn't been with a man in over a decade. Never did I put two and two together.

When my source entered the restaurant, she recognized me right away from my online pictures. After we said our "hellos," and settled in, she didn't waste any time delving right in, telling me she had worked for Preston for several months and how the two had become intimate with each other on several occasions. She went on to say that she was very troubled by the way Preston had dumped her personally and fired her professionally, both in the same day, without so much as a warning. She was never even offered a "goodbye" from Preston.

My source went on to say that she had come across sexual emails from Preston to Kirstie, while snooping through Preston's phone while Preston was passed out drunk. I recall chuckling to myself, picturing that scenario, wondering if my source was already planning on exposing Preston's secrets as she was going through her text messages. But who knows what is going on inside someone's head at any given time.

Opening her phone, my source showed me a couple of text messages from Preston to her. She went on to show me a picture of a text message from Preston to Kirstie, which appeared to specify that some sort of *code* was being used. When the message read "KP Duty," this was an indication, according to my source, that Preston was in the mood, probably drinking, and ready to play around. That is the message she received from Preston.

She replied to Preston by asking, "What time?" She never turned Preston down. During our interview, it was apparent that my source had deep, emotional feelings regarding her experience with Preston. It showed in her face and I could hear it in her voice. She went on to show me a picture of Preston and Kirstie in a tender embrace. It appeared that Kirstie was the dominant figure, according to what I saw in the picture, as she had her hands around Preston's waist while Preston gazed into her eyes.

I immediately knew that this picture could be worth a fortune and offered to help my source tell her story and even get paid for it. She added that once she realized that the two stars were hooking up every time Kirstie would visit, which was reportedly quite often, my source would be ready with her camera phone to capture the pair together. Of course, I was anxious to get copies of those pictures but my source was, understandably nervous. I would have to be patient. After all, my source was still hurting from the rejection she recently experienced.

We hung out for about an hour before saying goodbye. I suggested to her that she should call Preston and leave a message explaining how she had contacted me, and the National Enquirer, in order to expose Preston's secret life. It seemed likely that Preston would accept her calls if she knew her secrets were at risk.

I believe that is exactly what she did because I have only heard from her one time after that and that was to tell me she was no longer interested in moving forward with the story; she was sorry for wasting my time. I told her not to worry and I meant it. Although my source may have changed her mind, I had not; I will tell her story. Meanwhile, the truth stays hidden and just like Travolta, Preston is a master at deceit.

"She refuses to watch it and was less than happy when I came home from the shoot. I admit Kelly is a woman I would love to make out with in real life."

Adam Levine – (2006)

Referring to the way his wife felt about his attraction for Preston

Adam Levine

"She will be loved" . . . or will she? It would be over her infatuation and aching love for Adam Levine that Preston would eventually attempt yet another suicide. However, this time, it seemed she seriously wanted to die. Well, at least that is what Paula, an inside source, shared with me one foggy October evening. She described the hurt and sorrow Preston suffered once she realized that her love for Levine was unrequited. Preston had to come to terms with the fact that her dreams of him rescuing her from her imprisoned life, would never come to be.

Paula's position with the CoS, before her defection, was that of a *chaser*. She explained how it was her job to accompany a person, such as Preston, and be by his or her side practically twenty-four hours a day. Chasers were assigned to CoS members who were considered a high risk of fleeing the Church. Paula's responsibility was to stop Preston from defecting, something she said Preston tried to do several times.

79

"She was left completely devastated when Levine admitted to her how he admired her but was not in love with her." I listened intently as my source continued telling me the details of the attempted suicide, "The woman, who had climbed her way up the back of Hollywood, by sleeping with many of the leading men in town, was no longer the young ingénue. This realization left her soul dead. Sleeping pills and Xanax are a lethal combination for sure, but Preston swallowed at least two hundred pills that day, and I saw it all!"

Paula is also a registered nurse who assisted the CoS doctors whenever medical know-how was required, which is how she claimed to know all the details of the suicide attempt. She was the nurse on call the night Preston was found in the parking garage of the Scientology Hollywood Center. She explained how, on one of the rare occasions when she was not glued to Preston, Preston was found unconscious, by chance, by an attendant. If the attendant hadn't gone to the supply room when he did, it is likely that no one would have found the actress until it was too late. She most definitely would have died.

Apparently, the attendant noticed Preston's car parked to the side and he observed her passed out in the car. He then called the CoS authorities who rescued her and immediately transported her into the hospital within the center.

The medical team pumped her stomach and used the most up to date treatments to bring her back from near death. How is it that for the wife of Travolta? Everything would be done in order to keep her alive? Yet, when young Jett required medication for his condition, it was irresponsibly denied. Each extreme act done in the name of Travolta's career, *not* out of love.

Paula said Preston left an incriminating letter inside the car which was discovered after opening the car to get her out. Paula also conveyed how it was assumed that Preston believed she would never wake up from her suicide attempt, but of course, she did. In an odd twist, according to Paula, Preston was found wearing the same dress she had worn in the *She Will Be Loved* video, along with the same bright red lipstick she had on while making out with Levine. How unnerving is that?

Presumably, when Levine reached out to Preston to be in his video for the upcoming single, She Will Be Loved, a spark ignited within Preston that had long been extinguished. She became enormously obsessed with Levine and listened to his music around the clock, in preparation for what was soon to come. Paula was with Preston for the entire video shoot, which she said was exhausting due to Preston's numerous insecurities. She needed almost constant reassurance that she was still beautiful and desirable.

Preston managed to stay sober for the first part of the video shoot but was off the wagon by the second half. Paula alleged that Preston was also using cocaine to keep her appearing "up and bubbly," and to fool Levine and the rest of the crew into thinking she was sober. Apparently, she pulled it off. Days later, reality hit Preston that her time with Levine was coming to an end and, as far as he was concerned, it was just another job. When he originally cast her in the video, he didn't have any other intentions toward her.

Paula said it was common knowledge around the set that Preston and Levine had, indeed, hooked up; the chemistry was certainly there and Levine acknowledged having something of a crush on Preston. He seized the moment with the aging actress and fucked her, but it was merely a fuck to help get the video right, nothing more for him. Both the song and the video, Preston was sure, had been written for her personally by

Levine. She even confided in Paula how he had told her as much.

Recently, while listening to the song's lyrics . . . *"Beauty queen of only eighteen, she had some trouble with herself,"* and *"I know where you hide – alone in your car,"* I couldn't help but feel haunted by the anguish Kelly Preston must have been going through. After hearing, from her close companion, the details of Preston's obsession with Adam Levine, one might question if the words contributed to her emotional distress. Is that the reason she chose her car to act out a bizarre suicide attempt? That is a question only Preston can answer.

Paula reported how Preston had fallen hard, *really* hard, and required being on constant watch by several chasers; the CoS expected her to run and not come back. Sadly, Paula believed, Preston had been lonely for the attention of a man for such a long time, she had been swept off her feet by Levine, which ultimately ended tragically. Because she attempted to take her life over Adam Levine, after so little time invested, demonstrates what must have been going on inside her head. Too bad she doesn't seem to have the same energy to invest in her children. Preston's demeanor changed after this latest suicide attempt and she would never be herself again, as far as

Paula was concerned. She always appeared to be teetering just this side of a full blown emotional collapse. Preston had already suffered similar maladies twice over the course of her marriage, which were completely debilitating and took the actress several years to recover from each time. Those close to her knew that if she didn't succeed in ending her own life first, a third breakdown would absolutely do her in.

I have heard reports, from several sources, that Preston has been suicidal since first arriving in Hollywood. It has been said that she was always threatening to kill herself and it looks as if this attempt nearly worked. Regardless of what I've come to feel about this unhappy, deceitful woman, I can't help but feel sorry that she is so miserable with her life. It seems that she had been using the threat of suicide her entire life to get attention, as well as a lure to pull men in.

"I got caught playing doctors in my grandmother's garage,

but you know, it was very minor, just like sticking things in

the heinie."

Kelly Preston – (May 2003)

Quoted from Playboy Magazine

Subject: Kelly Preston Fucks Many!

This chapter title is the subject heading taken from the very first email I would receive regarding Preston's sex secrets. It pretty much says it all and the sender soon became a very revealing source for me. At first, I was skeptical, but after meeting with my new source, Fernanda, and hearing all the dirty specifics regarding a Travolta employee, whom both John and Kelly had sex with, it turned out to be a real treat!

As it turned out, the employee in question was Fernanda's own cousin. He worked for Preston for many years, two of which he had allegedly engaged in intercourse with the actress inside her home. Fernanda said her cousin had been bragging about it for years within the family. After learning about my impending book, revealing Travolta's sex secrets, my source was curious to know if I intended to delve into Preston's antics as well. Up until this first email, I actually had no inkling that Preston had any interesting sexual antics worth delving into, but that would soon change! I eventually heard from so many people concerning Preston, many claiming to know her extremely well from both the past and present. These people, who took the time to reach out to me, now had my full attention with their lurid tales of sex and infidelity.

According to Fernanda, her cousin would claim that while being intimate with Preston, the two of them always remained mostly dressed and that they always used protection. Her cousin also shared with her a juicy little tidbit about how the actress was also busy getting plowed by the gardener, the pool man, and several other property workers, as well as her personal assistant. It would appear that Travolta had definitely met his match in the kinky-sex-habit arena with his marriage to Preston.

Fernanda even had some extremely personal details reported to her by her cousin, such as how Preston liked it both ways – "In the pussy and up the ass," and went on say that, "he had visited both locations countless times." Once he and Preston would finish the deed, she would distance herself from him, "Until the next time she was in the mood for a good fucking."

One of the most outrageous stories shared with me was the tale of "Travolta Land." Apparently Preston began a fling with the chauffer and when John became aware of the relationship, he did not approve of her fucking any employees all by herself.

After all, if she were getting it, he wanted his share too! So, the chauffer, the actress, and the movie star partied together and had many nights of erotic sex. All bets were off! Fernanda said both "Kelly and John eventually grew to have real feelings for the chauffer" and, though they could not get enough of the sex, they had to fire him. No explanation, no goodbye. Just a final paycheck given to the chauffer at the gate by the security guard. This was clearly a pattern with the Travoltas' . . . or was it part of the Scientology way of life? Whichever it was, it seemed to be the same routine whenever they both dumped lovers. I believe it could certainly have something to do with Scientology philosophy due to the abrupt way that they sever ties with anyone whom they develop feelings for. It seems insane, to say the least.

That is exactly the way it ended for Fernanda's cousin. After a couple of years of having sexual relations with the star and occasionally screwing her movie star husband, he shows up for work one day to find that when he entered his security code at the gate, it did not work. He was then met by a security guard who informed him that he was no longer employed at the Travolta/Preston household. Fernanda explained that though it hurt her cousin at first, he confided in her later that it was the best thing that ever happened to him. He felt he had over stayed his welcome and how he should have left on his own years earlier. He stayed because the money was so good as well as the job being full of over-the-top perks. He knew he stayed way past his time. Fernanda concluded by saying her cousin asserted that, ". . . Kelly was a really good piece of ass and she definitely knew her way around a cock." She didn't bat an eye as she laid out the details of the affair before me.

My source wanted my assurance I would give Preston the same exposure that I gave her lying husband, John Travolta, and so I gave it. Admittedly, back when this journey first began, I could never have anticipated so many sources who would reach out to me with salacious tales from within the Preston camp. Only with time, would it become apparent that I was sitting on a literal treasure trove of Preston's dirty little sex secrets which she had been keeping for decades. After profuse encouragement from her ex-lovers, among so many others, I said, "Why not?" Why not expose her lies and cover-ups just as I have JT's?

"Has anyone ever heard the sound of Remini's voice or how opinionated she is?

Now imagine being stuck with her for three hours each month in a book club.

If you don't believe us, ask former book club member, Katie Holmes, if she's willing to join one with Remini again."

Kelly Preston – (2014)

Leah Remini and Ella Bleu

Even though leaving the CoS and defecting was hard on Leah Remini, it was minimal compared to what young Ella Bleu went through when Remini left. The two had become very close and Remini represented many things to Ella, most significantly, a friend. For most of us, friendship is something we are able to cherish for many years, but you see, Ella Bleu has only had Scientology *watchers* and *chasers* as friends her entire life.

My insider source into the Travolta daily household functions, claimed that if it weren't for Remini, Ella Bleu would have completely fallen apart after her brother Jett's death. If not for the love, inspiration, and guidance given by Remini through their friendship, the lonely kid may have been forever lost. I asked my source what the truth was behind the stories of how Preston treated the children. She told me that Kelly is basically an absent parent due to being a "drug addict who can't function anymore without being high."

My source's name is Sarah, and she was worried that something terrible was going to happen to Travolta's daughter. How it would likely turn tragic if she didn't get away from her mother and father, as well as The Church of Scientology soon. I asked her what she meant by that, to which she explained how children came up missing all the time within the Scientology walls. She feared that the CoS authorities were beginning to worry that the girl had now become a liability with her intimate knowledge of her parent's *true* life.

Allegedly, there had been several occasions when Ella Bleu had threated her parents to expose the truth of their phony marriage, if they didn't leave her alone. If they continued to require her to take classes at the CoS center, she warned that they were going to be sorry. Sarah went on to say that Remini had a way of keeping Ella Bleu calm and that it was because she really did love and care for the girl as if she was her own daughter. Remini only wanted what was best for Ella Bleu.

Sarah told me about one of the many rules instituted within the Travolta household, which was that Leah Remini no longer existed. Now a defector from the Church, she was dead to them. No one within the family was permitted to ever speak to her again; if they did, they better never get caught! Ella Bleu fell into a deep depression and gained fifty pounds. Alone and now without a true friend, this is what had become of the young girl who Travolta and Preston had been grooming with hopes of her stepping into the family business and becoming an actress.

Those dreams were all shattered when the child refused to continue in the spot light. In her few attempts at acting, she was not well received and the idea was shelved. This was done with much anger and animosity from her parents, which is how Sarah described the girl's experience. Sarah said, "I overheard Ms. Preston speaking on the phone one day while I was doing some work for her. The things she said about her daughter were extremely hard for me to hear." Sarah continued by saying, "Kelly was telling someone that she could barely stand to look at the girl anymore, and how she had become a constant reminder that her dreams were not working out the way she had planned."

Inexcusably, Preston was disgusted by Ella Bleu's weight and could not tolerate the sight of her "fat" child. Sarah concluded by saying, "She wanted to send her away from the home since she had turned out to be such a disappointment." I would consider all Sarah shared with me and even as she said, "I am leaving my position with the Travolta family, immediately, and moving back to where I came from," I could detect a real sense of fear from her.

It is easy to feel empathy for Ella Bleu, especially by anyone who has been made to feel like they were a disappointment to their parents. Imagine having your own mother and father look at you with disgust in their eyes – it would be enough to rip anyone apart – particularly a child. Hopefully, in time, Ella Bleu will find her way and be able to make her own decisions, living the life her brother, Jett, was not allowed to live. A life free from pretense. Every child deserves to believe they are loved and protected by their parents.

"Great man."

Kelly Preston — (2012)

About her ex-boyfriend, Charlie Sheen

Charlie Sheen, a Hooker, and Me

Imagine how thrilled I was to receive two emails, both sent to me from one of Charlie Sheen's porno girlfriends, with the message, "Charlie saw your story in the Enquirer saying how we shouldn't feel sorry for Preston. If you want to know more, you should call him." I called the number within minutes of receiving the emails, but to no avail. I tried again, no answer! I chalked it up to it possibly being a prank. Or perhaps he had changed his mind and didn't want to pick up when I returned the call. I was hoping to hear more about his involvement with Preston. After all, it was *he* who had attempted to contact me, or his latest girlfriend did. The email was signed "Capri," and I later learned that Sheen did, in fact, have a fling with the hooker/porno personality around the same time I received the email.

My upcoming book, *You'll Never Spa in This Town Again,* was beginning to make some noise regarding John Travolta and his wife. I was hearing from people all over the world who claimed to know them well. So many were reaching out to me, eager to share their personal stories of deception the couple had been portraying to the public. I was overwhelmed but decided, early on, to just go with it. I would listen to all who had something to say.

I attempted to call the number, sent by Capri, a few more times over the course of a several days but finally just wrote it off. Some months later, after Sheen went through his full blown, very public break down (which led to his being fired from *Two and a Half Men),* something told me to call the number again. I still believed that it was Charlie Sheen's personal number, and he had something he wanted to say to me. Oddly, I felt sort of flattered. So what if Sheen had been in a drunken stupor when he first reached out to me. I didn't care what the reason was, I was at a point where I wanted to hear his voice. Admittedly, I am a fan of the actor and found the whole experience to be exciting and rife with opportunities.

Why would the email say Charlie thinks we "shouldn't feel sorry for Preston?" I was chomping at the bit to find out, and my hunch to call again was about to pay off . . . big time! As I punched in his phone number, I kept wondering what Sheen may have wanted to share with me about his ex-girlfriend, Kelly Preston. My heart was racing as the phone rang.

"Hello?" It was him! I knew the minute he answered I was talking to the one and only Charlie Sheen, and he sounded buzzed. I took a deep breath before I responded, "Hello Charlie, this is Rob . . . I got an email to call you a few months back regarding Kelly Preston."

He replied, "Oh right, dude. You're the guy busting Travolta's sex life in the media"

I laughed and said, "Well, I do have a book coming out on the man."

"What's up?" He said.

I explained how I'm trying to find out what he was going to tell me a few months ago regarding Preston. "In the email, Capri told me you said I shouldn't feel sorry for Preston. I'm wondering what you mean by that." It was apparent he was partying during our conversation, as I could hear quite a few people buzzing around in the background. We were finally talking and even though he sounded high, he could not have been nicer to me.

I acknowledged being a huge fan, and also as being a regular viewer of *Two and a Half Men* since the beginning of the series.

He thanked me and said he appreciated the support, he then jumped right in with, "You know Preston shot herself. I was sure she had finally offed herself that time!" I just listened as he continued to talk. He then asked me to hold on for a minute; I had a feeling that was my heads up that he was about end the call, but he didn't. Instead, he went to a quieter spot where he said he could talk and hear a bit better. I was practically on the edge of my seat while he recapped details of the much reported shooting incident that had occurred back in the nineties. I was getting the story from the man himself, how fortunate was I?

As he spoke, I imagined he was talking to me from his home, but in actuality, I really didn't have the slightest idea where he was and I didn't ask. Here it is again . . . Preston threatening to kill herself! Sheen alleged how it was practically a common occurrence, for Preston to announce that she was going to kill herself. He emphasized that the episodes were usually motivated by either her career, love life, or looks.

"You couldn't help but love her back then . . . she had a certain quality that made you want to protect her." Sheen elaborated by saying, "I wasn't even on the same floor in the house when she tried to shoot herself, but I'm sure that had she succeeded,

I would've most likely been blamed. As it was, I still took a lot of the heat as if I had shot her myself! After hearing the shot, I ran to the bedroom to find her crying. Clearly, she had missed. She said 'I couldn't even kill myself right!' We just looked at each other and laughed."

He said Preston begged him to keep the truth of the shooting between just the two of them, and in those days, he agreed to her request. However, that was then and this in now . . . he no longer felt like he owed her anything, or like he was obligated to keep this story under wraps forever. All I could muster up to say was, "Thank you," for telling me his story and helping to clear up the *urban myth* surrounding the shooting. He stated that he planned on being more open and honest about many things that went down in the eighties and nineties. He was eager to clarify stories where the public believes him to be a certain type of person, and wishes for them to see the other side of him. The side *he* says is the truth!

Sheen concluded our conversation by saying, "My party is leaving – I gotta go. I hope you enjoyed the show!" I believe he was drunk (or whatever), but I was left a bit puzzled when he closed with that line. I guess when you're Charlie Sheen, you have a way of speaking that is all your own. Someone once asked me, "How do you know, for a fact, it was actually Charlie Sheen you were talking to?" To which I answered, "Trust me. When you're talking to Charlie Sheen on the phone, you know it's him!" (Refer to polygraph question # 8).

It would be only a few weeks from our chat that Sheen would be talking about the very same thing in his *Torpedo of Truth* tour. He was ready to offer up his realities and buried secrets to his show's ticket buyers. Speaking for myself, I was delighted to have had the opportunity to speak directly with the legendary man himself, and have an old rumor cleared up!

The bottom line: Kelly Preston attempted to kill herself, accidently missed and was apparently injured when the bullet ricocheted. Just another cry for attention?

"It is always sad when a marriage ends in divorce, especially for the children."

Kelly Preston – (2012)

About Tom Cruise and Katie Holmes

Katie Holmes

From the moment the Church of Scientology leaders selected Tom Cruise's next wife, Kelly Preston felt threatened. The Travoltas' had a long history of feeling like they played second fiddle to Cruise, and this new addition to the CoS family (i.e. Holmes) had Preston contemplating suicide yet again.

Not only were Travolta and Preston *not* invited to the wedding, but once the word was out about the new bride-to-be, they were also excluded from participating in any of the jubilant celebrations, which took place within the CoS. My source, Margret (one of Preston's chasers), said it was as if the "Second coming of Christ" had happened, as far as the CoS was concerned. Naturally, the fact that the Travoltas' were not invited, nor allowed to attend any of the gala events, was extremely difficult for Preston to cope with.

Preston was projected to have already fulfilled her purpose, with the CoS, of becoming a big star; a feat considered very doable due to her marriage to Travolta. Had she achieved her predetermined career, she would have been expected to recruit countless additional followers into the fold. When

Preston's career failed to live up to what the original CoS superiors had expected, she was placed in a subordinate position to Travolta. Margaret said he had such high hopes for Preston to carry her own weight and he felt terribly let down because her career never turned into anything that would help elevate their CoS position back to A-list standing. Word was that she was "limited," which helped explained how she was only useful for the marriage smokescreen. There wouldn't be any more time or money invested in Preston's career – it had been written off as a total loss. It seems just about everybody was fed up with Preston and her needy ways – she was considered extremely high-maintenance.

Meanwhile, Katie Holmes had her name in the media as Tom Cruise's future wife, and the world, was eating it up. Preston continued downing the pills and chasing them with vodka, according to Margret. In fact, Preston actually thought the vodka was undetectable on her breath, which is why it was her beverage of choice, her "essential accessory." She was only fooling herself. Margret described how, "You could tell a mile away whenever Preston was drunk, which was just about every day, just by her attitude. She would be obnoxious and sloppy; she couldn't hide it from any of her superiors and was repeatedly called onto the CoS carpet to be reprimanded." I listened with intent interest as Margret continued, "She was holed up in a hotel suite, partying with one of her lesbian lovers and doing drugs. That is how Kelly handled being shunned from the Cruise and Holmes wedding." It was 2006 and the holidays were just around the corner. The wedding was going to take place in November and Preston wanted to be as far away from the event as she possibly could

Travolta knew exactly where she was, and for that matter, so did the CoS leaders. They even knew what she was doing, after all, she still had her *chasers* with her most of the time. Sadly, no one really cared as long as Preston didn't do anything to embarrass the CoS or any of the attendees. There was always the underlying dread that she would try another stupid suicide attempt for attention.

Margret acknowledged that when she had left the CoS's control, the Travoltas' were in a lot of trouble with the VIP's. "When I was leaving, John had been given a thirty-day sentence of solitude by the Church because he could not keep Kelly under control." Margret said when his sentence was passed down, "Travolta hit the roof!" She was thankful to be defecting at a time when she feared that she would have been stuck watching Preston around the clock; something Margret said she couldn't stomach doing another minute. After all, she had already spent several years as one of Preston's personal chasers and knew just about every dirty detail there was! It was easy to see why my source would be happy to be leaving her responsibilities with the Travoltas' behind, along with what she referred to as, "a life of nightmares." I agreed with Margret that when it's time to leave, you'd better get going while you are still able.

Toward the end of our discussion, I asked my source why she thought Preston was so "fucked up," given the prestige one would assume she had within the CoS. What about the CoS's educational opportunities and personal growth development? She answered by saying, "Kelly had never spent one minute reading or doing any classes within Scientology and that she was only a member through her relationship with Travolta." I believe after hearing these bizarre details about this peculiar woman, we have come closer to knowing the real Kelly Preston. What a mess!

"Don't ever stop fucking me!"

Kelly Preston – (1996)

Her line in "Jerry Maguire"

Tom Cruise

Kelly Preston was promised the moon to step in and save Travolta's rumored gay life. One of the perks for parading around the globe as his dutiful wife (beard), was an exclusive, three picture deal; she was earmarked to become a star. Preston had joined the Church of Scientology after Tom Cruise. When she was offered the sweet part in "Jerry Maguire," she was, understandably, beyond thrilled. Not only did she land the role of a lifetime but she would be spending a lot of time with Tom, who my source, Ellen, revealed was actually Preston's dream man. It certainly was *not* Travolta, who she knew was a full blown homosexual even before the Paris marriage. She also learned that her husband had absolutely no intention of ever faking *anything* with her whenever the cameras were not rolling.

Travolta made it clear to his young bride that Tom Cruise was not interested in her *at all,* and that he would no longer tolerate her now infamous antics with drugs, pills, and alcohol. If she were found to be bothering Cruise, Travolta would have her sent away to a camp in Arizona, along with the others who were disobedient. There, she would be punished and cleansed (more like brainwashed). Ellen said, "Kelly did her best to heed the warning John had given her. But it was all happening just a few weeks after Kelly had to tolerate John's New York boyfriend being in town for a month." Ellen continued, "How much could one woman take? She thought she knew what she was getting herself into from the beginning, but she had no way of knowing John was not only a raging homosexual, but also a sex addict who was pretty much a lost cause."

Preston had plenty of desires of her own, for both men and woman, but at that point in time, she wanted Tom Cruise – and it was pissing Travolta off. Not so much because he cared, it was more because he didn't want to be embarrassed by his drug and alcohol addicted wife. Allegedly, Cruise was enjoying all the attention from the wife of Travolta, who was at that time, a higher ranking Scientologist. He even went so far as to really toy with Preston's emotions while filming. In other words, he started blatantly flirting with her. However, as it was later revealed, the flirtations were all a pretense as part of his *method acting* because he wanted the chemistry between the two of them to be believable on screen. Preston was already known for her immature approach when it came to men and love, and in this situation, she was true to form. She was on a mission to get with Cruise sexually, and she thought he felt exactly the same way about her.

The sex scene, when Cruise's character is fucking Preston's character, according to Ellen, ". . . was a very difficult shoot. The reason was because Kelly kept over holding the scene due to her pent-up passion for Tom – she wouldn't stop kissing him, even after the director yelled 'cut!'" My source told me about the time she accompanied Preston and Cruise on a dinner engagement, which Preston actually thought was going to be the start of an affair. In reality, as Ellen pointed out, as far as Cruise was concerned, it was all about getting the chemistry right for the film. "I guess when you are acting out scenes where you are having sex, it would make sense for the stars to have chemistry."

On the way home from the dinner, Preston confided to my source that she was over the moon with the possibilities of her and Cruise becoming sexually involved, and all that could come of such a union. It seems Preston had forgotten that this pairing of the two stars was only part of a prior commitment Travolta had to fulfill from the original marriage agreement with Preston.

Ellen explained, "Kelly was already trying to figure out how to manage all the possible problems she saw coming. She talked about how John was going to handle the news when he learned that he was wrong about Cruise's feelings towards his wife. This little charade of Tom courting Kelly went on for a full two months before they started shooting the film. By then, Kelly was head over heels in love with the star. Kelly even asked me, 'When do you think he will tell me he is leaving Nicole for me?'"

Watching the scene where Jerry Maguire is arguing with Preston's character, you see how angry Preston is – and that is "100% authentic," according to Ellen. Just minutes before they shot that scene, Cruise had Preston summoned to his dressing room, where he was sitting with his then wife, Nicole Kidman. Preston later recounted the incident to Ellen, telling her how when she walked in, she was expecting a glorious moment alone with Tom. What she got instead was a devastating shock, for as soon as she entered into the trailer she saw Kidman sitting next to Cruise. Cruise opened by saying to Preston, "I need you to clear up some things to Nicole for me, please."

"Like what?" Preston asked.

"You must tell Nicole that we are *not* having an affair and that it is all just a lot of idle gossip."

Preston did as he asked and went a step further by adding, "I love my husband, John, very much."

In reality, Preston was seething at that exact moment. All she could think of was how much her admiration and infatuation for Cruise had instantly turned to hatred. Outwardly, they all laughed it off as so much Hollywood drivel. Right then, the knock on the door came, "Five minutes on set Mr. Cruise and Ms. Preston!" Cruise and Preston then departed the trailer, leaving Kidman inside waiting for Cruise to return after shooting the big break up scene.

My source acknowledged that what happened next, Preston could never have seen coming. While walking with Preston to the set, Cruise stopped her in her tracks, looked her right in the eye and said, "I have something to tell you." Preston just stood there, not knowing what to expect. Ellen remembered Cruise telling her, "Your husband makes me sick! He is a homosexual who is living a lie and I can't stomach being around him . . . or you! I look forward to the day when I never have to be around the two of you ever again."

Preston continued to listen in pure horror. Once he had his say, Cruise started to walk away, but instead, he turned back and continued his outburst toward Preston, "I was never interested in you, this has all been a joke to fuck with your head. Now, you had better hit your mark because I am only giving you one shot. No retakes! You either get the scene right the first time or you won't be in the movie – we already have your replacement on standby."

To say Preston was totally livid would be an understatement; she had taken the bait and been played for a fool. All the while, Cruise and Kidman were having a big laugh, at her expense, behind her back. Determined to be the consummate professional, Preston made her way to her mark – the director said "action!" and action is what she delivered. Preston pulled it off in one take, which was relatively simple since the scene between her and Cruise involved them fighting. She was supposed to hate him in the scene – and hate him she did. In fact, according to Ellen, that same hate stayed with Preston from then on, or at least for as long as she worked for Preston.

Once the scene was shot, Cruise walked over to Preston and said, "Good for you! You have just secured your part in the film. Now get out of here!" She would, in fact, get out of there immediately, and as soon as she saw Travolta, she told him of the dirty trick Cruise had played on her. She even told her husband how much she now hated Cruise and Kidman. Sadly, she received absolutely no sympathy or solace from her husband and he acted as if he couldn't have cared less. As Ellen tells it. "I witnessed Preston go through so much while filming her few scenes with Cruise and it always took a toll on her. She was bedridden practically every day at the end of each day of shooting."

Just when Preston thought she had seen the last of Cruise, the studio ordered several retakes which would require the two of them to finish together. Although the film was a huge hit and Preston pulled it off without a hitch, it would change Preston in many ways. People around her began to notice how, now that she had made the film and got so many rave reviews, she was careful to never be so naive again. It didn't go unnoticed how, whenever she saw Cruise and Kidman coming, she would dart in another direction in order to avoid any contact with them.

For a brief moment, it looked as if Preston might become an important actress of interest, what with the film doing so well and many critics praising her performance. But it was not to be. She would be back to facing reality within no time; back to the way her life was actually going to play out. Both on the big screen and in the real world.

"I have talked with Kelly and told her to get out of her marriage and come to Nashville and start a new life away from the man with all the gay sex rumors circulating Travolta, but she won't leave."

Nicole Kidman — (2013)

Nicole Kidman

Even before Nicole Kidman had met or married Tom Cruise, Kelly Preston didn't like her. In the early days, the two had their fair share of bumping heads around town, when they were auditioning for the same roles. The fact that Kidman had been an insider within the CoS, and was already entrenched in its way of life, left Preston feeling as though she had, once again, been a day late and a dollar short!

My source, Anita, claimed that as soon as Preston was brought into the fold of the CoS, "Kidman made it clear that *she* was the queen bee and that she and Tom would in no way take a back seat to John and Kelly." Anita added, "Everyone, including Kidman, felt the same way – the *real* stars at the top of the movie industry, and in the Church, were Tom and Nicole. When Travolta started getting noticed for his antics, like getting caught having sex with men, which humiliated Kelly, Nicole never missed an opportunity to throw it in her face."

During an award dinner, at the Scientology Hollywood Center, honoring both Travolta and Cruise for their outstanding work recruiting civilians into the cult, Preston and Kidman were passing each other in the hall. According to Anita, Nicole loudly shouted at Preston, "It's a real shame that you can't keep John under control. He keeps getting caught by the tabloids running around town having sex with men." There is little doubt that Preston heard her loud and clear, as most everyone inside the building could have heard Kidman's Aussie accent echoing through the halls. They all probably felt the same way.

Cruise and Kidman played by the rules, they did not have the embarrassing stuff, such as bedroom infidelities, out there for all the world to see. Kidman could not have known the hurt and disappointment Preston must have felt every time John was caught with another man. The only time Travolta would want to be seen publicly with his wife, was for a staged family outing. Anita believed that, "Nicole knew what it was like to be treated like a queen and to be cherished by her gorgeous, movie star husband. In front or behind the cameras, and during their most private moments, Nicole was loved, adored, and put on a pedestal by Tom."

"Kelly, on the other hand, knows what it is like to be the butt of everyone's jokes." Anita went on to say that the way she saw it, "She hears the whispers as she passes by, which has to be painful. She handles the hurt doing what she has always done – she runs from the issue straight to a bottle of booze, often accompanied with cocaine and sex with a man, or a woman, to help fill the emptiness inside her."

Living the empty existence that is Preston's daily routine would be daunting on even the most hardened drug addict/alcoholic. As it happens with everyone, Preston is aging. Her system cannot handle the abuse and bounce back as quickly as it once did. There was a time when she could go without sleep, (with the help of some hefty cocaine use), for as long as a week. When she was ready to come down, she would do it with Vicodin. She would then sleep endless hours, waking up to binge eat everything in sight for several days. Anita also witnessed how difficult it was for Preston to watch from the side lines, the careers of the three big movie stars, (Travolta, Kidman, and Cruise), skyrocketing, while her career tanked. Even with her three-picture deal, it was understood that, between the two of them, it was Kidman who was the shining star – an actress of critical acclaim. Whereas, Preston was pretty much only famous for being Travolta's beard and now for having a child with Autism. She had to accept that she was going to spend her days trying to hide from the CoS, the media, and pretty much the whole world.

When she had reached her wit's end, Preston went on a crusade aligning with high ranking CoS officials, as well as the bottom feeders, in an effort to get everybody on board to vote for Kidman's removal from the CoS. Anita claimed that she was not sure what leverage Preston had in order to influence anyone's decision, but that Cruise was completely aware of what was going on because he had already procured Kidman's replacement. Anita added that when the decision was made for the marriage of Cruise and Kidman to come to an end, and the secret votes were being cast, Travolta and Preston voted countless times. They even enlisted the help of their CoS friends to assist with stuffing the ballot box to ensure the outcome would be favorable for them. According to other sources, Kidman confirms that is pretty much the way it went down.

My source, Anita, explained how she came to know this information: it was all in the Tom Cruise file she had stumbled on, and had the presence of mind to copy, in the 1990's. The notes laying out the plan to get rid of Kidman where all there. Anita said, "They had been bugging her phone and recording the conversations. When they got what they wanted, they approached Tom, who seemed to take everything presented to him at face value. He walked away from a woman he truly loved. Problem was, he loved his career, and himself, more than anything else." When the CoS convinced him that Kidman was a problem, as well as a liability, it was agreed that she had to go.

Miraculously, Cruise bounced back quickly. In fact, he was bouncing on Oprah Winfrey's couch just as soon as he received the greenlight from the CoS that he could share his big news with the world. He announced, during his famous display of jubilation, that he was head-over-heels in love with the beautiful, young Katie Holmes. Cruise had been pleading for permission from the CoS to tell his fans of his love for Holmes; when he finally got the approval, he was eager to share his exciting news on Oprah's show. The tricky part was that since the go-ahead had come just hours before the taping, there wasn't adequate time to get the announcement scripted, so he adlibbed. Nearly every person on the planet knows what became of that! His spontaneous decision to shoot from the hip, resulted in his career taking a huge hit after that fateful episode of The Oprah Winfrey Show aired. He would be mocked relentlessly, by all the talk show hosts and just about every comedian in the business. It didn't take long to realize that he never should have acted so impulsively, but as Anita put it, "He didn't take time to compose himself and the rest is YouTube history."

When Kidman was ultimately expelled from the CoS, Anita believed that it was then that the Travoltas' felt they had a chance at regaining their rightful position as the CoS's golden couple. It was Preston, however, who was busy plotting some sort of reconciliation with the now available Cruise. At that time, she was completely clueless to the fact that Cruise was already in love with his new, future bride. She soon had the opportunity to meet Katie Holmes and immediately felt as if she, once again, had the rug pulled out from under her. Preston was seething because the same man who had hurt her so deeply while filming "Jerry Maguire" was breaking her heart all over again. According to Anita, Cruise had been the source of so many of her problems, to the point of her blaming him for keeping her from achieving her ultimate dream of super stardom. Preston vowed, loud enough for Anita to hear, "'I'll get him good – you better believe I will!' She then passed out drunk."

It would appear that Nicole Kidman has never looked back with any regrets about leaving the CoS, nor the *dream marriage* she may have thought she had at some point. The public has seen her build a new life with Keith Urban and their two children. Interestingly, her two adopted children from her marriage to Cruise, Isabelle and Connor, both chose to defect from the CoS the minute they were of legal age. They have also reconnected with their mother, after Tom Cruise prevented her from being with them. Those kids loved and missed their mother and now that they were old enough to make their own decisions, couldn't wait to reunite with her.

Anita concluded by adding, "I have copies of the documents which prove that Kidman was legally forbidden to talk about many secret conditions contained in the divorce settlement. I am thrilled the children are back with Nicole!"

"He gave me a ride on his Harley and I was hooked."

Kelly Preston - (2003)

Referring to ex-fiancé, George Clooney

George Clooney

Learning about Preston's relationship with George Clooney would be a fluke. I happened to become close friends with one of Clooney's previous assistants who, I learned, had worked for him around the time he was involved with Kelly Preston. My friend, who was also my source for this information, validated what I had already learned regarding the famous actor and the troubled actress. True to form, it was her neediness and insecurities that would eventually destroy another desperate attempt at a normal relationship.

The story reported to me was that long before meeting John Travolta, Preston fell really hard and fast for Clooney; she wanted desperately to marry him. Reportedly, that is one of many reasons he wanted to get away from her. What man wants to hear the word "marriage" after one week of dating? Even though she had only been divorced from Kevin Gage for a short time, Preston made it abundantly clear to Clooney that *she* was the marrying type, and ready to get back on the horse – or as my source put it, "Back on the Harley."

According to my source, Preston became pregnant with Clooney's child shortly after they started dating. She even showed him a sonogram photo as confirmation of the impending birth. This turn of events would help her to get closer to Clooney which she would use to her advantage. Of course, there would never be a baby born between the two, as Preston would ultimately announce that she had a miscarriage during the third month. Once Clooney found out he was off the hook, he broke it off with her and never looked back. Imagine the sense of relief Clooney must have felt when he realized the major bullet he had just dodged. My source added that the day Clooney told Preston it was over, he actually through a huge party to celebrate the end of his horrifying nightmare. There were some who claimed to know that the pregnancy story was simply a ruse that she had used to trick Clooney into a more lasting union.

Preston was beside herself, she did not take the break up well at all. Within a few weeks she would attempt suicide. According to the details I learned, it was the onset of what would become a way of life for the actress – booze, pills, and multiple suicide attempts. The hopes and dreams of a young girl from Hawaii had been reduced to a sequence of shallow, unhealthy relationships. She was now an emotionally disturbed woman who abused prescription drugs and alcohol - one whose lifestyle was taking its toll.

While they were a couple, it had been reported that Clooney purchased a pot belly pig for Preston. However, my source informed me that it was actually the other way around – Preston presented Clooney with Max, the pig. She demanded him back after the break up. Clooney's former assistant explained that, "Preston buys Clooney this cute little pig and when they break up she wants it back. Clooney told her to go to hell!" In fact, he would go on to enjoy many years of happiness with the pig given to him by Preston. Undoubtedly, she loved Max and by taking him with her, Max would help secure a bond between her and Clooney. Or perhaps it was out of shear bitterness. In any event, Clooney must have breathed a huge sigh of relief for making it out relatively unscathed from that relationship. Putting that chapter of his life behind him, he would go on to become a huge movie star, often shadowed by the same gossip that followed Travolta – is he gay? The rumors have continued throughout his career, even after he finally got married.

"I'm a big fan of her . . . and her music."

Kelly Preston – (2008)

Referring to Lisa Marie Presley

Lisa Marie Presley

Preston's *girl-crush* on Lisa Marie Presley was reported to me from several reliable sources. It seems she would make it known to anyone within ear-shot how she would love to crawl into bed with Elvis' daughter. Preston was in awe of Lisa Marie's talent and status in the world, and wanted desperately to add this fellow Scientologist to her growing list of conquests. My main source, Linda, knows the two through her affiliation with the CoS. She said Lisa Marie could not stand Preston and had absolutely no interest in having a lesbian relationship with her.

Lisa Marie was reportedly going through some tough times, in her then current marriage, when Preston started *being there* for her. Though Lisa Marie didn't like her in that way, she still used her as a sounding board for listening to her marital problems. Linda attested that, "Lisa Marie knew damn well that Kelly had launched a campaign to get her into bed, during their conversations of homosexual desires over coffee." Linda said that, although Preston had made it clear to everyone that she wanted Lisa Marie sexually, she now found herself wanting even more from Lisa Marie – kind of "a girlfriend with benefits." Linda presumed that she wanted a mutually reciprocated relationship,

Preston's birthday was coming up so she invited Lisa Marie to go with her to the lake for some rest and relaxation. Of course, Preston had a hidden agenda. Lisa Marie did meet Preston at the lake house with her kids in tow, and made it clear the minute she opened the car door that she would, "not be licking any pussy!" that weekend. Certainly not when her kids were with her; if Preston couldn't accept that, she would be leaving. Preston did accept the terms, according to my source, and so they all stayed in the lake house for four days, without incident. Preston had even managed to remain sober, with the exception of her normal pills – which she needed on a regular basis, in order to function.

While Preston spent the weekend on her best behavior, in an effort to impress Lisa Marie, she became even more deeply infatuated in with her. She would shortly become so obsessed, that within a month, after the lake house trip, they would never speak again. According to Linda, the way Preston went after the object of her desire was "completely relentless." It was obvious that the methods she was using to gain the affections of the legend's daughter were definitely not working. My source went on to say that those two almost "came to blows," one evening during a Scientology function at the Hollywood Center. When Preston, who was drunk at the time, saw Lisa Marie arrive with her husband, she totally lost it. She apparently threw a hissy fit, on the side lines, and told people how she was going to be a thorn in Lisa Marie's side until she got what she wanted. A meeting was called by the CoS leaders to figure out how to put an end to Preston's bullying of Lisa Marie. It was made crystal clear to Preston that if she made even one more move toward Lisa Marie, she would be excommunicated from the CoS, and never allowed any of the luxuries that she enjoyed being Travolta's beard.

Linda continued by saying that once Preston realized her obsession was dangerously close to costing her what little she had left, she decided it was time to pull the plug on her quest for Elvis' daughter. "Sure, she fell hard for Lisa Marie," Linda said, "but just because Preston wants something does not mean she is going to get it, no matter who she is married to. It's about time she figured that out."

When Lisa Marie Presley left the CoS, Linda initially believed the reason was due to her issues with Preston. In the end, however, there were, reportedly, numerous reasons why Lisa Marie left. Mainly, she needed to get her sanity back, Linda said. "When you wake up and realize you are destroying everything you touch through Scientology, you're lucky if you are able to get out!" It appears that Lisa Marie made it away from the CoS *and* Kelly Preston's crazy obsession for her. Linda also claims to be among those who are lucky – those who got out. I have heard from others who don't consider themselves so lucky; some of my sources are still trapped within the confines of the CoS. They have reached out to me with the most heart wrenching stories I have ever heard, most expressing their desire to escape what they refer to as "a cult."

"I work tirelessly beside my husband to make the Jett

Travolta Foundation one of the greatest foundations ever!"

Kelly Preston – (2010)

As retold from the previously published *Tracking Travolta,*
September 30, 2014:

Jett Travolta Foundation

The Jett Travolta Foundation was set up by the deceased child's parents, John and Kelly, in an apparent, pathetic attempt to turn all the attention away from the despicable, inhumane way they treated their son, Jett. Many people were outraged upon hearing how the Travolta's referred to their son's disease as "Kawasaki syndrome". They must have really believed that, like all the other things they have rewritten regarding their lives, they could now tell the world this wad of bullshit about Jett's condition, and we would believe it!

The correct question to ask about how they handled the death of their son should be, "How far can two people have their heads up their own asses?" The media was not buying it and neither were their fans. The internet was abuzz with everybody talking about what horrible parents they were for the way they treated Jett. To deny him proper medication, which would have probably stopped any seizures from killing him, was absolute NEGLECT on both their parts. Then, to donate ten percent of the Jett Travolta Foundation to Scientology, the very Church whose beliefs may have helped kill him? It is so sad that Kelly and John did that to their child. It was only while on the witness stand in the Bahamas, John Travolta finally admitted his son had Autism. Well, if that doesn't speak volumes on the kind of father Travolta was to his boy, I don't know what does!

For me to have witnessed Travolta engaging in all the lewd acts I wrote about in *You'll Never Spa In This Town Again,* the acts of homosexuality, a thing The Church of Scientology has no tolerance for, showed me, up close and personal, that he is a hypocrite as well as a sexual predator.

I used to cringe when I would hear Travolta describe how *his* Jett had gotten sick from all the carpet cleaning he did during those early years, because he was such a clean freak, (so he said). He was not such a clean freak when I personally witnessed him down on his knees, in a dirty, fungus infested steam room, sucking on a big, fat cock!

As far as the 2010-2011, Jett Travolta Foundation tax returns are concerned, there has not been one dollar given to anybody, or anything, regarding Autism.

According to the website, Showbiz 411, the foundation has reportedly given out 57k since conception. Really? All I can ask is . . . WTF? The parent's love for their son sure shines through in black and white; 57K when you have so many millions? Seems to me, he should have established Jett's foundation with a minimum of one million dollars. But as I have already stated, this foundation was Travolta and Preston's answer to a public relations crisis, *not* a beloved son's death. The proof is public domain. To have actually witnessed, first-hand, Travolta's mistreatment of his son was utterly disturbing, to say the least. I knew when John was inside the spa, masturbating with this guy and getting their germ infested, sauna love on, that he was an unfit father. If the authorities had witnessed his behavior that day, Travolta would have made world news with a sex arrest, due to his son being with him. He really lucked out again that day. Can you imagine when George Michael was arrested in Beverly Hills, that infamous day, if he had a sixteen-year-old relative with him, while cruising the bathroom like a sexual predator? Or, how about Pee Wee Herman's scandalous sex arrest for getting caught playing with himself in public, at that movie theater? Can you imagine if he had had a sixteen-year-old relative along with him? Well, that is exactly what daddy John Travolta did when I witnessed his parenting skills, on January 11, 2007. He was hooking up in a public spa, while his son was with him! That was a very sad day, to witness that little, lost boy looking for his missing father, who was *busy* in the spa. Very sad.

It would be great to see, in time, the Jett Travolta Foundation really stand for something good and true, but it is doubtful that day will ever really come. The smoke screen, established after Jett's death, will likely fade into the dark, just as their ill-fated child did while left alone for so many hours in that bathroom during that fatal night. As the years since Jett's death have proven, there is very little interest or love coming out of this foundation. The response we saw, was the immediate, alleged fake pregnancy of Kelly Preston. It is true that they had a baby, but I have it on good authority, that she did not deliver or carry that baby herself. Anyway, to replace a child, just like that, shows you how this couple thinks. I can only hope, by the time baby Benjamin is Jett's age, his father will have his sexual addiction, (the one that caused him to make so many poor choices regarding Jett), under control.

"Anti-depressants are turning kids' into walking time bombs.

Eight of the last thirteen school-shooters were taking

prescription drugs.

We can no longer sit back and let the clock tick, waiting for

more deaths, suicides or people driven to violent acts by

psychotropic drugs."

Kelly Preston (2005)

Appearance on "The Doctors" November 20, 2012

When this particular source, who shall be called Beverly, sent me an email filled with details about Preston's appearance on the TV show, "The Doctors," I was deeply entrenched with my slander law suit against John Travolta and his attorney, Marty Singer. At that time, my name was frequently in the tabloids due to stories from my Travolta books. As a result, I was receiving many daily emails from various sources claiming to have more secrets detailing the lives of both Travolta and his wife, Kelly Preston.

Beverly was eager to share what she knew, however, she requested that I not divulge where she worked because it could cost her in ways I could only imagine. That is why I have changed her name and must be somewhat vague concerning some of her details. I have honored her wishes – for her safety. But I'm still going to give you the dish!

Without beating around the bush, Beverly came straight out and said, "Kelly Preston was so high while taping her segment on the daytime show, The Doctors, that she nearly fell over on stage several times." She suggested I log onto YouTube and watch Preston's segment. I encourage my readers to do the same. Beverly pointed out that while watching, I should pay special attention to her demeanor as she is talking, "There are clearly certain points where you can see she is on something." That something, my source clarified was "Cocaine and Xanax." Reportedly, Preston is addicted to the way the two different types of drugs hit her system.

I can reveal this much, my source was in a close enough position that Preston confided in her how she was under an enormous amount of pressure to get the segment, for ABC, right. "It had to go off without a hitch." she repeatedly told Beverly. Preston expressed her fear of retribution from the CoS if she "fucked up again." It seemed as if this was the way they, (i.e. the CoS leaders), expected Preston to get things done these days . . ." fucked up."

Beverly kept telling Preston, ". . . remember you're an actress, you can do this – just go out there and act!" Preston was practically climbing the walls because she hadn't had a drink all day and for her to go for even an hour without a drink is really saying something. "I can't do this anymore . . . I need a drink!" Preston kept saying. So they gave her a total of four drinks to help settle her down. That, I'm told, is the number of shots it took before her eyes rolled back in her head and she said, "Now you're talking!" Beverly said it was the third shot that brought Preston back to life, but it was the fourth that sealed the deal for the actress. She was now ready to hit her mark.

What proved to be a big problem for Preston was the fact that there were countless delays during the taping of the show. By the time they actually shot her segment, she was "jonesing," big time. She was barely able to get a grip on her emotions or body. After viewing the YouTube video, it really does look like Preston is all fucked up and not behaving like a sober person.

It was Beverly who said that Preston had become "unscripted," and that she was unable to get a grip without her "script," along with a drink. That is when I got the idea for the title of this book, as it all started to make sense to me. Watching Preston on the show, I noticed how she acted kind of crazy – the way she articulated some words, and the angle in which she held her head while talking. She seemed to have the pronunciation, mannerisms, and posture of a person who is high and at a loss.

Beverly claims she helped Preston pull it together enough to get through the taping, but as soon as it was over, she came unglued. Leaving the studio, Preston was poured into an SUV where she immediately went crazy. She was crying about how she was in big trouble for messing up the show, due to her substance abuse. She screamed for her flask — she would not be under control until she was good and shit-faced.

"I can't believe we actually made it through the shoot!" Beverly concluded, "I couldn't handle that woman anymore. I will be away from her soon enough." The next time I spoke to Beverly, she said she was, indeed, long gone and out of the "thick of it." She is now happy with her new life and new peace of mind, and intends to keep it that way.

"She is just like her father; she loves the spotlight . . . she is

our little actress."

Kelly Preston – (2005)

Ella Bleu Travolta

I spent years reinventing myself before my initial meeting with John Travolta, as I wrote about (in great detail), in my previous book, *You'll Never Spa in This Town Again.* The very first thing he said to me that day was that the child that he and his wife, Kelly Preston, were expecting was a girl. He went on to say that, as of that moment, no one in the media knew the sex of the child — so naturally, I felt honored, and special, that he would choose me to share this information with. However, inappropriately enough, the next thing Travolta would say to me was that he wanted "to suck my dick." I recall being taken aback when he mentioned his unborn daughter and sucking my dick all, in the same breath.

The Travolta's have always been very good when it came to public relations, doing things like putting out fires. However, they are horrible with follow through. Awkwardly for them, the internet has recorded all of their public deceptions. Anybody with a computer can access the web to see for themselves what a couple of frauds those two are. An excellent example would be their PR attempts to repair their reputations for the child negligence, which lead to the death of their first born son, Jett. They wasted no time and immediately established a foundation for their deceased son in his name. Disappointingly, that was pretty much it!

Young Ella Bleu must be aware of many of the secrets within her parent's phony marriage. She also must know what her older brother, Jett, had to endure during his short, sixteen years of life. Such as being denied medical attention, as well as the medicine he desperately needed in order to have a fighting chance. Suffice it to say, it looks as if Ella Bleu is now the keeper of the secrets within her famous family. Only time will tell if Ella Bleu will have the strength to reveal the truth of the fake marriage, and all she and her brother had to bear, for the sake of their celebrity parent's reputation. One can only imagine – shades of *Mommy Dearest?*

Many of my sources expressed concerns and were extremely saddened about the life Ella Bleu lives. Some believe that this child will be a total mess as she gets older, pointing out the way Preston outwardly felt about her daughter's appearance. Her disappointment that she was gaining so much weight. As of August 5, 2015, Ella Bleu's website, which promotes her as an actress, has sat dormant for at least half a decade. My source explained to me that, "This is exactly how John and Kelly do things – they put their energy into Ella and her potential to become an actress (though she never wanted it), and when it didn't pan out, they just moved on. They never bothered to stop and think about what they were doing to their child. For that matter, did they care!"

Another source explained how, "Kelly lives in a dream world, where her daughter is perfect and she will not accept anything less. She leaves the little girl's website up because *that* is the child she loves . . . not the actual person she has become; the child with an eating disorder and full of issues." Preston has absolutely no patience for people with weight problems, especially her own children. Jett was also overweight and out of shape due to his lack of attention and proper care. The same thing is happening to his younger sister.

This same source went on to say, "On her web-site, Ella Bleu tells us that her fans mean everything to her, and how she loves to be in touch with them." It sounds great but it is far from being true, according to my source. One can only imagine how heartbreaking that situation is. It appears that Ella Bleu has been conditioned, almost like something out of an old Hollywood movie. It seems so very sad – this child doesn't even have true love from her parents, let alone fans, my source told me. "Ella Bleu is beyond miserable and wants nothing to do with stardom, or her parent's lies anymore!"

Anyone interested in seeing the child Preston fantasizes to be her daughter, can visit her official website at www.ellableu.com . You will find that it is pretty much a shrine to the daughter Preston wishes she had. In my opinion, they should take down the damn site and let the child live what time she has left as a child, in peace. If you Google it and it's down . . . they got the message.

While I was researching this book, I received many emails regarding Ella Bleu. Some wrote about the way she must have felt when she saw her parents, in an apparent PR stunt, replace her beloved older brother, Jett, so quickly. I wanted to share some of the comments, from a few of the people close to the Travoltas', who reached out to me:

"When my dog died, I couldn't bear to think about getting another one for several years. I cannot believe the Travoltas' have already produced a new boy to take the place of the defective one. The one they never would accept."

"Their daughter must be going through hell! Can you imagine what is going on in her head regarding her brother's death? I'll bet she realized how she could be replaced so quickly too! They are horrible parents! They actually allowed their son to die all alone in a bathroom!"

"I can only wonder what their daughter, Ella, is going through with her brother just dying, and being replaced – just like that!"

"Ella Bleu has never had anybody to turn to for love, with the exception of Leah Remini, but she was ripped from her life without any warning. That little girl took it really hard."

Just like her older brother, Ella Bleu had yet to meet her grandmother, another of my sources revealed. The girl finally did have the opportunity to meet her grandmother when Jett passed away. It seemed Linda Carlson was brought in for damage control; she made a few statements for the press in an attempt to help the cover up, for the death, go off without a hitch.

I hope with time, this young, innocent child is able to find her own way in a world filled with all the lies in which her parents have smothered her. Similar to Nicole Kidman and Tom Cruise's children, who left the CoS just as soon as they were old enough to make a rational decision on their own, Ella Bleu may follow in their footsteps. Once she is of age, she can build a life all her own — a life not based on lies and deceptions for the sake of stardom and Scientology. Time will tell if she is able to move on and become independent. After all the brain washing from her parents and the CoS, have they succeeded in irreversibly breaking her spirit? I wish only the best for her!

"Nobody should have to lose a child. It's unfathomable.

But I'm here to say that you can get through it.

You can live again."

Kelly Preston — (2012)

The Big, Fat Lie

The big fat lie was Kelly Preston's promise to build a school to save the world . . . the school that NEVER happened! "We saved our son's life." Read the cover of Redbook magazine, July 2002. Right there, on the cover, Preston tells the world how wonderful the both of them are for all they had done for their child, Jett. She boasts about how, (due to their superior status as human beings through the Church of Scientology), they wanted to share with the world just how magnificent they were. It's tragic that, as of 2015, that same child has been deceased for six years. It is a fact, that the Travoltas' truly did have the power to save sweet, innocent Jett Travolta's life from his horrifying fate. But instead, they elected not to do the right thing by allowing him to die.

It is extremely difficult to read the full magazine article, as it is blatantly filled with falsehoods, which are now coming back to bite the Travoltas' in their asses. Their secrets are easily coming unraveled. When one looks back at old stories from, for example, six years ago and compares the same stories with today's version, one can clearly see the deceit the Travolta family continues to put out to the world.

Preston goes on and on in the Redbook article, about her "big green school," she is building, and how she has personally raised over five million dollars toward construction costs. She continued by declaring how she is determined to raise another twenty-five million for its completion. The fantasy school *never* came to be . . . because she was full of shit!

Preston was known to boast about how she home schooled her son and how he was so healthy, knowing all along that Jett had Autism and *not* Kawasaki disease. Jett needed medication specifically for Autism, and seizures, in order to stay alive. Instead, she decided to be deceitful, in an effort to make herself appear to be a good, caring mother. In fact, she was, and still is, an unfit mother who let her son die due to parental neglect. Preston refuses to publicly acknowledge her first child, Trent Gage, who she had with then husband, actor Kevin Gage. Trent has been swept under the rug in the name of her Scientology beliefs, as well as out of sheer vanity.

These days, Ella Bleu has put on a lot of weight, most likely from all the neglect and insanity that goes on in her parent's lives. It seems, the young girl is eating her way through her emotional troubles. I am told, by inside sources, that now her parents are looking into having Ella Bleu undergo Lap Band surgery. That way, she will appear more presentable in public. *Not* because they care about her weight for health reasons; they are more interested in having an attractive, slim child who can carry on with the family tradition of acting.

Both parents were terribly ashamed by Jett Travolta's appearance. I was repeatedly told by my sources that they were embarrassed to the point of PhotoShopping many of his pictures. Most everyone has seen the very public, close-up picture of Jett kissing his father. Of course, it is completely "shopped" to make Jett look more like his father; even more than Travolta than Preston would have liked. It seems to me, that when one truly loves a child unconditionally, any imperfections would not be an issue, especially to the point of PhotoShopping them away.

"Rest in peace, Jett," is what one of his uncles said to me while remembering the way Travolta treated his now deceased nephew. I asked what he would do differently now to save Jett, and he answered, "I should have called the authorities on John and Kelly to have them both arrested for child neglect and endangerment!" He was noticeably upset by the tragic loss of Jett, and his helplessness at getting Jett away from his parents. He said it still haunts him to this day.

The feeling I came away with, after reading the Redbook article, just as I have with other articles featuring Preston, was . . . repulsion! She could have changed so many lives with the truth about Jett's condition, but instead she selfishly opted to change only her and Travolta's bank account. She continued to lie to the world about all things Travolta, forsaking even her children, while limiting their chances for living anything resembling a normal life.

The *unscripted* lives of the Travoltas' is now an indelible part of history thanks to the ever expanding database of information available on the internet. They no longer have the power to prevent the truth from coming out. The internet has also made it very difficult for their spin-doctor attorney, Marty Singer, to manipulate what the public sees and hears. With all the big, fat lies exposed, a flood gate has been opened, revealing these self-absorbed, self-serving, and just plain selfish celebrities. With each passing year, we see more of who they actually are: Actors – playing the role of their lives! It is a shame they couldn't do it right. Many people could have been spared a lot of unhappiness and pain.

"Ya know, I'm glad to see someone has the balls to come out and show what a predator JT is.

I worked with him for ten years on set and, boy, did I see him ruin lives!"

Mark Riccardi – (2010)

Exclusive stunt double to John Travolta in fourteen films: sending me his congratulations for standing up to Travolta

Mark Riccardi

As previously published in my 2013 book, *Tracking Travolta*:

Exclusive stunt double and coordinator to John Travolta [and first-hand eye-witness to Kelly Preston's "unscripted" life]

When I heard from Mark, I had no idea who he was but it didn't take me long to know I had hit the jackpot with this email. One of the highlights of Marks early stunt career was when he began as a stunt double for Jonathan Frakes on Star Trek "The Next Generation." This was the start of a long career for Mark as a stunt man, which eventually led to him working with John Travolta as his exclusive stunt double, stunt coordinator, and 2nd unit director during Travolta's amazing comeback trail.

After all, Mark worked on so many films with Travolta. This was a man who really knew JT and was an employee too, I had penetrated Travolta's deep inner circle.

Up till this point, I was hearing from men who had slept with the star and were either happy with John or not, but this was the first from a bona fide ten year employee. To be John

Travolta's stunt double is quit a title, with all the credits to show for it, and that is exactly what Mark Riccardi was.

Unfortunately, Mark has been "Travoltanized" into the corn field, more about that in a minute. I was beyond excited to hear what this true Hollywood insider had to say about Travolta.

The first thing Mark said to me was that, I said it best when I called Travolta a predator and that he had witnessed John destroy so many men that he had slept with, Mark was upset and it came through the conversation in his tone of voice.

I came away from our first chat, feeling sorry for Mark for the way Travolta had treated him or better said, not treated him. I truly believe Mark cared for Travolta and was more hurt than anything when he got fired. He felt that Travolta was sick of looking at him, knowing he had so much information on him and was canned.

It was very exciting, listening to Mark describe the scenarios he witnessed with his boss. After all, Mark had been in so many Travolta films: Michael, Get Shorty, The Generals Daughter, Face off, Primary colors, Phenomenon, Swordfish, A Civil Action, Broken Arrow.

All in all, Mark was in around thirteen Travolta films as his stunt double or his stunt coordinator. He really knew John [and Kelly] inside and out. When I first heard from Mark, I Googled him to see if he was the real thing and boy, was I pleasantly surprised to see he was indeed!

When Mark sent me his first unsolicited email about Travolta, he called his boss a predator. He claimed to watch John destroy many men's lives. Here he was again destroying lives, but this time I'm hearing it from this big time stunt double to this big time movie star.

So we agreed to meet for coffee at Coffee Bean on Sunset Blvd in West Hollywood, I was excited to meet this man who portrays Travolta in a body double way.

Mark is a very good looking man in person, much, much better looking in person than Travolta is. I bet that's why John fired him. When you look at Mark you feel like you're looking at a good looking version of Travolta, then when you see Travolta, you think 'jeez, he should be the stunt double, not Mark.'

We spotted each other immediately, he commented on my resembling JT and how he couldn't get over what he had seen Travolta do to guys in all the years of working side by side with the star. He told me all about a project he was working on called "The Mamaluke," and he was happy with his life away from Travolta, but that he had secretly hoped that JT would someday rehire him.

After all, as Mark said, up till now with you, I have never talked about John and his secret sex life with anyone before. He said he felt compelled to reach out to me and congratulate me for having the balls to stand up to his old boss, the predator.

When he said I said it best when I called Travolta a predator, I knew Mark was being totally open and honest with me. He is definitely straight, but man! If he wasn't, he would certainly be busy with pursuers of the male gender.

You see, Mark is the one thing that no matter how hard Travolta tries to act the scene out, he is not straight and it shines through when you watch him, whereas Mark is the straight version of the movie star, so he is really what we all fell in love with in all those Travolta films. The presence of Mark's heterosexuality is what John drew from for all those movies for a decade.

We drank our coffee and talked. We sat there for about an hour. I let Mark get years and years of BS with Travolta off his chest. There were no less than five guys that Mark said he witnessed Travolta destroy after he was done using them for sex.

I used to think of the Mile High Club as a club you joined when you had sex in the air. After hearing what Mark had to say about John up in the air having orgies and getting fucked by numerous men in the back of the plane on their way to some glamorous location, I will never think of it again the same way.

Mark claims Travolta was much more discreet in the early years, but as the years rolled by, John became much loser with his discretion.

Apparently, many things about JT became looser as the years passed. He told me of the gifts Travolta would shower on his love interests, houses, cars, boats, jewelry, you name it! Mark claimed John purchased it for the men of his desires. I found this information to be a sharp contrast to what I had heard all these years about how cheap John was with all the masseurs. I guess John does have a generous side, if you are someone he has a crush on or wants gay sex from.

Besides hearing this information from Mark about all the gifts Travolta showered on these men, I had never heard anything like this.

He also elaborated on Travolta's wife, Kelly Preston, telling me she knew everything about her husband and that she was completely fine with it. After all, he said, she is gay too. "She and John have a fake marriage set up to fool all his fans."

Mark said on many of the trips they would take in the plane, Kelly always had her girlfriend/ assistant with her. He went on to describe Kelly as a pill -popping drunk, and that most of the time when he would see her, she would be in a stupor.

He also said she was an extremely cold woman who had a lot of unresolved issues in her life and they had caught up with her and it was really taking a toll on her. Travolta would often tell Kelly "Just Take A Pill" and walk away from her needs. Her Mothering skills apparently were "nonexistent" and they had nannies to do everything.

"She needs to sober up," he said. Maybe then she would be a better Mother, but until then she is always wasted and hiding behind her substance abuse. He went on to point out to me that when Jett Travolta died in that bathroom in the Bahamas, that

poor Jett had been laying there for over thirteen hours alone and dead.

"That is the kind of Mother she was," the kind that could have a son with special needs and she couldn't stay sober long enough to help her child stay alive.

Mark didn't tell me anything about Kelly that I had not already heard many, many times by family members to her, and by past relationships she had with people who reached out to me to share their stories of Ms. Preston and her secrets.

We had been talking for quite some time, when Mark got a call regarding his upcoming new project and he needed to take it, we said our goodbyes and parted.

On my drive home, I thought of all the stories Mark had shared with me about his adventures with the Travoltas' and what a great book it would make. I came up with the title "Confessions of John Travolta's Stunt Double." As Mark said, he was thinking of writing his own book about all the years being employed by Travolta and what he went through.

I didn't know it at the time, but that is one book that will never make it to the light of day, due to the fact he was employed by

Travolta in one way or another, and as we have seen with Doug Gotterba (the six-year boyfriend), if you were employed by Travolta, you are going to be shit out of luck because of the confidentiality agreement.

In December of 2013, Dish Nation did a promo for my upcoming book "Tracking Travolta."

In their piece, they mentioned that Travolta's stunt double had contacted me, and was going to be included in this book when it came out.

Just days later Mark Riccardi was "Travoltanized" again!

His Twitter account was shut down, and everywhere I looked Mark had been vanished into the corn field by John. His website was gone, all mention of Travolta had already been removed from Mark's life.

Months earlier, when Gawker ran a piece on 4/2/2013 titled "Grease Money Document shows John Travolta's insurance company paid more than 84k to handle sexual assault allegations," and in the piece, Marks name was mentioned as putting in a demand for money.

From that time on, when I checked out Mark's sites and social media, all mention of John Travolta had been removed.

Once the Dish Nation piece ran later that year and Mark was mentioned, he has now completely vanished from sight in every way connected to Travolta.

When you work for John and you sign an agreement not to talk, you can't, that is what I have learned, good thing I never worked for him. I hope someday Mark Riccardi shows up again in social media, till then though Travolta has shut him up.

John has silenced him, but he can never remove what time has already written regarding Mark Riccardi and John Travolta, [and Kelly Preston], *though for now it looks like Travolta has won again and "Wiped Away" a life, he hasn't.*

I hope Mark stays strong and has a great life, he is a really nice guy. And I want the world to know what Travolta did to him. I had a lot more I was going to share with you regarding dirty sex stories Mark witnessed and shared with me, but I decided not to. I don't want to add further to the pain Travolta has already brought him.

Since this is a true story, I could not omit Mark from this book, though there was a time when I was still on the fence about it, but when I saw Mark had broken his own silence by putting in the claim for damages that Gawker wrote about, I knew he would understand, since he opened that door.

Now that John has silenced Mark, at least the world can know about it through me, since he will never be able to write about it himself, and who knows, maybe someday I will write "The Confessions Of John Travolta's Stunt Double."

After all, it is juicy and filled with ten years of Travolta's homosexual hook ups and lies. Only time will tell

UPDATE: *I am happy to say that Mark is finally back up and running with his social media life, but like I said earlier, he has been "Travoltanized" and all mention of Travolta has been removed from his life and his web site and all media accounts that Mark had, have removed Travolta's name.*

UPDATE: 2015 — I felt it was important to include this previously published chapter from *Tracking Travolta* in this book, as it contains relevant and true references to Kelly Preston, which include some of her many demons. Because

Mark was around Preston for nearly fifteen years, this is obviously a man who got close enough to witness the truth!

Not included in *Tracking Travolta*, is the following information as told to me during my Coffee Bean conversation with Riccardi. He revealed a bit of what he was privy to regarding Preston. Aside from the great detail he went into regarding her many drugs of choice, some of what Preston was hooked on was Vicodin and Xanax. I asked him how he knew the exact drugs she was taking and he replied, "She made no bones about what she was using! If she was in a bad mood, she would say, 'my pills haven't kicked in yet . . . give me a minute!'"

He went on say that, what concerned him most about Preston was the way she drank booze while on pills. When traveling with her on the plane, he had witnessed her overdose more than once. I asked him to elaborate on that topic, for instance, did she come close to dying? He laughed and said, "Not usually, not when you're a drug addict like her. She OD's all the time from over self-medicating, but once she throws it all up, she's back in business." However, during one of the trips he thought it was the end of the line for her. She had apparently been unresponsive to whatever they were doing to get her to vomit, and for a minute, it looked as if she wasn't going to come out of it. She was dying right before his eyes. When I asked him what Travolta was doing while this was happening, he answered, "John was in the back of the plane, getting fucked. He had no clue what was happening to his *wife* at the front of the plan."

Epilogue

I honestly wanted to come away from this experience with Kelly Preston on a positive note. I had hoped to uncover a side of her that I would enjoy, respect, and find to be warm and friendly. But that side of the woman was a no show throughout this entire endeavor.

Not a single person who contacted me, out of the hundreds of emails regarding all things Travolta, had anything nice to say about Preston. My sources were jaded. They felt belittled, and kicked to the curb like garbage, by Ms. Preston, as soon as she was finished using them for whatever her momentary fantasies, or drug-induced pleasures called for.

When I started this journey, to learn the truth, which connected me to the Travolta's back in 2008, it was never intended, in any way, shape, or form, to be the outing of John Travolta. Nor was it to be the revealing, inside look into Kelly Preston's unscripted life. The purpose was simply to tell my personal story surrounding my own actual experiences at the private health spa where I had been a member for over fifteen years. I had a lot to tell.

After a vicious, physical attack on my life, that took place at City Spa in 2003, the owner, through his negligence, allowed me to go through yet another beating by the same man, just months later. Adding insult to injury, the owners would further insult me by telling me that I was no longer welcome to use their facility.

Soon after I recovered from the head trauma, mental, and physical issues, the idea to write my memoirs was suggested by my best friend, Lorrie Llamas. Lorrie believed it would be a great source of therapy to help me come to terms with the horrific ordeal. It was made very clear that all my years of loyalty to the spa added up to nothing, as far as Kambis, the owner was concerned. I met many celebrities and formed many friendships throughout my membership years and I had kept my mouth shut about all I witnessed. However, if they were going to treat me like this . . . I'll give it right back to them.

I titled the book, *You'll Never Spa in This Town Again,* and set out working on it. When news spread through the media about my impending book release, I was drowning in emails sent from countless people, claiming to be closely associated with the Travolta family. It seems that no one, up until me, had ever challenged John Travolta regarding his adulterous, and openly homosexual behavior, while cruising the spas.

Suddenly, it was me that countless victims of Travolta's sexual assaults would turn to for help. Within a few months, I heard from many people upset with Preston as well. It didn't take long before it became clear that I would need to include Preston and the whole fake marriage scheme. There were numerous cover-ups, intended to dupe the public into believing the lies about the Travolta's marriage. It was time for them to be exposed.

I learned from my previous efforts that putting together a book can be a grueling experience. I truly dreaded the process of writing this book, even when I had originally added it to my to-do list. Unexpectedly, when the time came to actually sit down and get started, I enjoyed it much more than I could have ever imagined. I just wish my subject, Kelly Preston, could have turned out to be the hero, if not for the public, at least for her children, but that was not the case.

Addiction is a terrible thing, as Preston has repeatedly admitted in countless articles and television shows. She knows what she's talking about because she has been a drug addict her entire life, as well as a drunk. Unless playing a scene in a movie, she lives a life not showing any genuine attention to the people who need her most . . . especially her children. The only place to go from there is to tumble further downhill, unless she is someday able turn things around.

Did she settle or did she hit the jackpot? The answer is evident . . . she most definitely settled. If Preston had lived a life of sobriety it would have changed everything. I would like to think that if she had been sober, she would never have sold her soul to the Church of Scientology for a sham marriage and a posh lifestyle with a famous actor, trying desperately to hide his blatant homosexuality. It stands to reason, that if sober, she would have likely thought twice before agreeing to give up her dignity and allow Travolta to embarrass her daily, by flaunting his boyfriends in her face, by way of magazines and the internet. Most importantly, if sober, she would have surely made wiser choices regarding her son, Jett. The range of more positive outcomes for the circumstances she has endured, is extremely broad in scope.

I feel very confident in saying, John Travolta and Kelly Preston will undoubtedly maintain this fake *marriage* to the bitter end. It doesn't matter which one leaves this world first. Death, it seems, will be the only way Preston will ever be free from the chains keeping her bound to the CoS, Travolta, and her many addictions.

Sadly, for all that she was or could have been, in the end, she is simply a minor character; a B-list actress playing a bit-part. For as much as she had focused selfishly on her own ambitions for fame and happiness, she isn't even the star in the story of her own life. Bottom line: Diana Hyland was John Travolta's first *beard* – Kelly Preston will likely be his last!

THE END

Acknowledgements

First and foremost, I would like to profoundly thank all my sources who made this book possible; those who took the time to contact me and share their experiences. To the family members, friends, ex-lovers, former employees, and various other eyewitnesses of Kelly Preston: your courage motivated me. Your willingness to speak out helped inspire me and gave me the strength to tell your part of the story. In addition, a shout out to all the Travolta and Preston fans who reached out to me just to say a friendly "hello!" Thank *you* so very much!

To my very dear friend, Terry Lane. I have been blessed with your friendship for so many years – I pray to have you by my side for the duration of this ride called life. You said you would be here for me and I'm holding you to it. This book would not be possible if not for you! I am a work in progress with my books and you know the obstacles I have had to endure to get my thoughts into written word for the world to read. You stepped up and rescued me. It is essentially because of you, *Kelly Preston: Unscripted* is complete. Please NEVER forget that you mean the world to me!

Thank you, Robert Lane for all the effort you put into creating the cover for this book and perfecting my new trademark logo. You truly worked your magic and exceeded my expectations.

To Ocy Hinkle, I appreciate all you do for me as my friend, you have helped me in so many ways over the years. I can always count on you! Thanks for all the support and help with my books, from files to original book cover designs, you have assisted me so much in this process.

To G. Scott Sobel, Esq., you are a true friend! Thank you for all your advice and guidance into this new chapter of my life, I look forward to many years of friendship.

To Charles Karpinski, a friend to me since the tender age of eighteen. I love you so much and I could never take for granted all you do for me on a daily basis. It is because of your love and support; I have survived so many storms in my life.

To Francine Smiderly, I truly value the friendship and loyalty you give to me and my girls.

To my three girls, Dali n Dazi, and our newest addition, Abbi. I love you very much and because of you, I have had the wisdom to make so many good choices for us. I'm blessed for having you as my babies. Also, to my three birds, Little Joe, George of the jungle, and Picasso II, you sing to us all day and we love you for it!

To Lorrie V. Llamas. How can I thank you enough for showing me what I am worth and for giving me my girls? I think of you every day and hope I am making you proud. I'm certain you are dancing with the angels in heaven and keeping a protective eye on us – we feel your presence!

Finally, I want to thank all the people who have come and gone in my life, helping to make me the man I am today. Friends and relatives from the past, as well as everyone in between from then till now – you know who you are and you know the part you played in my life. I thank you for it!

SPECIAL BONUS

WORLD EXCLUSIVE

RAW AND UNCUT!

DOCUMENT PACKAGE

Kelly Preston: Unscripted

Print | Close Window

Subject: RE: Preston
From:
Date: Thu, May 07, 2015 11:10 am
To: info@youllneverspainthistownagain.com

Robert,
I hope you will be exposing the truth about Kelly's girl action. I was a bartender at Peanuts lesbian club in LA for about three years.
Kelly was a regular for a while. She always came in with a group of gals and never went anywhere in the club by herself. One evening she showed up at the club alone.
She was a mess and before I knew it she was being carried out by a couple of big broads? I think they were Scientologist, When Kelly saw them come in to get her she completely went white in the face. Later that evening one of the patrons in the club was bragging that she had made out with Kelly before she got so wasted. Sad situation and she seemed trapped to me.

Best to you!

Subject: Your story in the mag
  From: ███████████████
  Date: Mon, Oct 25, 2010 ████████
    To. "Info@youllneverpainthistownagain.com" <Info@youllneverpainthistownagain.com>

Hey, we saw the story in the Enquirer. I'm sending this message for Charlie, and he said that we shouldn't feel sorry for Kelly Preston. LOL. If you want to know more, he said just give a call. (Charlie Sheen, of course!)

Capri
█████████████████

From: ████████████████████████

To: authorrobertrandolph <authorrobertrandolph@aol.com>

Subject: RE: National Enquirer Kelly book

Date: Wed, May 6, 2015 8:19 am

Congratulations!!

Saw the story on your book in the tabloid and was wondering about the Kelly Preston book you are putting out. My question for you is do you know she is bisexual and spends many nights at her girlfriends house?

The two have been spotted all over the neighborhood here convorting and enjoying each others company. I think what you are doing is to be applauded. I want you to focus on Kelly's sex life as she has one that is very active...You must already know all these well known facts.

Keep up the good work.

Susan moore

Print | Close Window

Subject: kelly
From:
Date: Wed, May 25, 2011 1:33 pm
To: <info@youllneverspainthistownagain.com>

dear mr randolph,

ive been keeping an eye on your book that's coming out. its all over the web and even in the national enquirer. i wanted to contact you and to let you know i know for a fact that you are telling the truth about john travolta.

i was wondering why you haven't mentioned anything about Kelly. like where is she and what is she up to when he is at the spa and then it dawned on me that you didn't say anything because you probably don't know. after all your book is about him and other celebrities going to the spas and so on so why would you look into kelly.

well mr Randolph, you may not know what shes up to but I sure do. im considering sharing my secrets about those two with you if you are interested. you have another book coming out i read somewhere. tracking the travoltas or something like that. maybe you could use my information for something in the future. are you interested in hearing about kelly and her lesbian life style? or is the book only going to be about her husband and his sex secrets? yes, i said lesbian. shocker isn't it?

so why am i telling you all this. Well, i have plenty of information i would be willing to share with you. i have known Kelly for a few years and we were extremely close. not just as girls who hang out together, but sexually. everything was fine until one day she up and decided she never wanted to speak to me again. So yes im scorned, if that's what your thinking. who wouldn't be? so what do I have to gain, whats my angle? i want to be compensated for the information i have to share with you. you can use it in your book, or whatever. that is up to you. think on it and let me know if youre interested. in the meantime i do ask that our communication with each other remain private.

Sincerely

Print | Close Window

Subject: Book available??
From:
Date: Sun, Dec 04, 2011 9:12 pm
To: info@youllneverspainthistownagain.com

Hello Robert Randolph,

I have been following your exposure of John Travolta in the media and wanted
to ask if you are aware of the long running sexual relationship between Kelly
Preston and Kirstie Alley? I have seen a lot of stuff while working for Ms.
Preston and after being fired with no explanation, I am ready to talk and share
pictures and text messages to prove what I am saying.

I have always remained loyal to Kelly and never thought I would actually try and
out her to the media. She is bi-sexual, not gay, I know this because for a very
brief time, she and I were intimate. I knew in my heart that it would not last and
when she first made it clear to me she was interested in sex, I was flattered.
Since I am a lesbian, I was excited.

Things became uncomfortable between us over the last few months; a couple
of weeks ago, when I went to her home as I do off and on, since I was working
for her, I was not allowed on the property. Instead, I was met at the gate by
security who gave me a final check and said I was being let go.

That was it, no explanation or a personal goodbye or anything. I have tried to
reach her repeatedly but she has written me off. I would like to talk in person
with you.

Thanks

Kelly Preston: Unscripted

Print | Close Window

Subject: Charlie and Kelly
From:
Date: Mon, Sep 13, 2010 1:50 pm
To: <info@youllneverpainthistownagain.com>

Mr Robert Randolph,

I have been following your story in the National Enquirer regarding your book "You'll never spa in this town again" I'm excited and really looking forward to reading it. With that being said let me come right out and ask...are you interested in hearing about Kelly Preston? Trust me, she is no saint in that marriage.

If you are, I've got an earful for you. Unlike most who would pilfer it, I don't want anything for it at all. Well, except anonymity.

Omg, let me just tell you. Kelly has been sleeping with women for years. She is not into men at all. That's all smoke and mirrors for her career and her image. I'm known K. for years. Way back when she was with Charlie Sheen.

I had met her through a girlfriend of mine who was a call girl during the late eighties. My personal favorite era. Anyway, my girlfriend would go to Charlie's house for work, if you know what I mean. Sex, yes sex. I thought she was crazy for escorting. She was still my girl and she used to tell me the most outrageous stories. Back to Kelly. So yeah, my girl told me on her very first visit to see Charlie and handle their "business", Kelly joined in and they had a threesome. I was like, get out. She went into detail and everything. After reading about your book and checking out your website I think they were BOTH sex addicts. Apparently Kelly isn't the type that, you know, just lays there.

I read somewhere that you feel sorry for poor Kelly.....ha, this is a women who needs no one's pity!!! Remember how I told you I liked the 80's? Well, hearing about Kelly and Charlie in detail reminded me of those penthouse forum stories that you always wondered whether or not they were true except in this case, I was getting the story right from my girl who made sex her living.

I preordered your book and can't wait to read it. I hope it's as juicy as the stories my girl used to tell me.

I also hope you are being careful for your safety. I've heard some scary stories about scientology and how it's a cult, etc.

If you'd like me to elaborate on the stories my girl used to tell me, I'd be more than happy to share them with you. Let me know if you are interested.

Take care.

From: ▓▓▓▓▓▓▓▓▓▓▓▓
To: ▓▓▓▓▓▓▓▓▓▓
Date: Thu, Feb 23, 2012 12:22 pm

Mr Randolph,
I have been following your story in the National Enquirer regarding your book youll never spa in this town again.I'm excited to read it.I'm wondering if you are interested in hearing about Kelly Preston? Trust me she is no saint in that maraiage..

I have some things I could share with you but I do not want anything for it
Except amanibade

Kelly has been sleeping with women for years she is not into men at all (except for her career) I first met Kelly when she was with Charlie Sheen. I have known her for many years

I first met her through a girlfriend of mine who was a call girl during the late eighties my girlfriend would go to charlies house for sex and on the first visit Kelly joined in and they had a three way.

I read somewhere that you feel sorry for poor Kelly.....Trust me this is a women who needs no pity!!!

I hope you are being careful for your safety.

Please let me know if you are interested in hearing more.

▓▓▓▓▓▓

Kelly Preston: Unscripted

5/22/2015 Workspace Webmail :: Print

Print | Close Window

Subject: kelly preston fucks many
From: FERNANDO ████████████████
Date: Tue, Dec 14, 2010 4:59 pm
To: info@youllneverspainthistownagain.com

I have family member who worked for the travoltas for many years. while he worked for the family, both john and kelly wanted to fuck him. my cousin chose kelly because he is not gay. anyway, he screwed her for almost a year and he said he was not the only one screwing her. she is fully aware of john's gay activity but they have an agreement. i know this to be true i can't give the sources. kelly preston likes to fuck just as much as john does

Print | Close Window

Subject: Re: kelly preston fucks many

From: FERNAND —

Date: Wed, Dec 1 5, 2010 1:10pm

To: info@youllneverspainthistownagain .com

Robert,

All I know is they snuck around and had numerous quickies. Apparently Kelly and John have an agreement, not necessarily an open relationship but an agreement, he goes off and does his gay thing and she knows about it, as long as it is not bluntly in front of her. She on the other hand has screwed a handful of men ranging from all ages and walks of life. Nothing lasts very long because of the situation but just about any man would willingly fuck her. Although John keeps getting the shit end of the stick, she's just as guilty as he is, they're both unfaithful and they know it. Because of who he is and what he's worth, coupled with Scientology, there's an agreement they will stay together. As strange as it may sound, they really do love one another. Also, I was told Kelly is not a great mom, she's too focused on herself and her career, I am not sure what career? They've got a few nannies for each kid, you see how well that worked out.

My cousin does not know I sent this out to you and I kind of feel bad about doing so. But he bragged about it and how she initiated it. He said she's not even a good fuck either but being who she was, it was very exciting. She then would distance herself from him afterward, until she wanted him again. They always used condoms and almost never fully undressed.

I just think she needs just as much exposure as him. I always read about what a poor thing she is and how she does not know, it's all hollywood bullshit.

Kelly Preston: Unscripted

Subject:
From: mark riccardi <stuntd███████████
Date: Fri, Oct 29, 2010 7:43 pm
To: "info@youllneverspainthistownagain.com" <info@youllneverspainthistownagain.com>

Ya know I'm glad to see someone has the balls to come out and show what a predator JT is. I worked with him for 10 years on set and boy did I see him ruin lives. The only thing that kept me from exposing him was the fact I was getting paid very well. When he fired me in 2002 I am sure it was because I was too over exposed to his hook ups and seen many things. Anyway I look forward to your book and I would consider giving you info but would remain anamous.

From:
markriccardi<stun
10:14 am

Date: Mon, Nov 08, 2010

To: info@youllneverspainthistownagain.com

You know basically all I can say is that from working with him I was privey to the behind seens actions that the public rarely seen. Though he never came onto to me and just flirted at it there were times on many flight across country were him and his secuurity side kicks would be macking it up in the back of the plane. These particular guys were always around and I know for a fact they were sharing the same bed as I spent a weekend at his home in Maine and slept 3 doors down from his room. I meanwhile put a chair up aginst my door to inadverlty keep him from visiting! :) Because of him and having the power I've seen him ruin probly 3-4 guys . I mean mentally send them into depression and nevrous breakdowns because of his actions. I think u said it best he's an out right predator..because he feeds on liasons with who he is (his co called hollywood power) and then showers them with gifts ie motorcylces ,luggage trips rolexs money loans I've seen it all bro. I could write my own book. Anyway I know most of the guys he didled with and they have since moved on all with nice hush money big checks, me of course I got fired because I seen to much and him lookin at me knowing what i new became uncomfortable....Anyway Im sure u heard many of these types of stories but this one comes from the inside and is very real...l really liked Kelly and never could belive he would do her that way but to me its that kind of relationship thats says she's cool with it....No way she could not know...

~~t~~and sure I would love to have a book. thanks bro I wish I had the balls to come out   with this years ago but I was kinda in the mode that maybe he would take me back......but never did. now l;m left with great working memories but they are soured by his exploits and his other stupid advances and his misdeeds. Anyway theres other stories but theres really no need to go any further it just feels good to
express the BS i had to deal with with someone who too has been exposed to JT advances.

&

1J1ark

204

Kelly Preston: Difference between revisions

From Wikipedia, the free encyclopedia

Revision as of 10:21, 18 May 2012 (edit)	Revision as of 01:58, 23 May 2012 (edit) (undo)
ClueBot NG(talk | contribs)	0zero9nine(talk | contribs)
m (Reverting possible vandalism by 173.126.4.63 to version by Symbols100. False positive? Report it. Thanks, ClueBot NG. (1082320) (Bot))	(→Personal life)
← Previous edit	Next edit →

(11 intermediate revisions by 2 users not shown)

Line 11:	Line 11:
| years_active = 1980–present	| years_active = 1980–present
| spouse = [[Kevin Gage (actor)|Kevin Gage]] (1986–1988, divorced) [[John Travolta]] (m 1991–present)	| spouse = [[Kevin Gage (actor)|Kevin Gage]] (1986–1988, divorced) [[John Travolta]] (m. 1991–present)
| children = Jett Travolta (1992–2009) Ella Bleu Travolta (b. 2000) Benjamin Hunter Kaleo Travolta (b. 2010)	| children = Preston's first child she had with her first husband Kevin Gage the child is disabled. Preston has three children with Travolta (1992–2009) Ella Bleu Travolta (b. 2000) Benjamin Hunter Kaleo Travolta (b. 2010)
| alma_mater =	| alma_mater =
| website = http://www.kellypreston.com/	| website = http://www.kellypreston.com/

Line 35:	Line 35:
==Personal life ==	==Personal life ==
Preston was married to actor [[Kevin Gage (actor)|Kevin Gage]] from 1985 to 1987.<ref> [http://articles.chicagotribune.com/2005-07-30/entertainment/0507300256_1_kelly-preston-celebrity-psychiatric-drugs "For Kelly Preston, life is more than 'Sky High'"], "[[Chicago Tribune]]", July 2005 </ref> She also had a relationship with [[George Clooney]],<ref name="yahoo" /> who gave her [[Max (pig)|Max]], a pet pig that he kept after the couple split up.<ref>{{cite news |title=Grunt in peace, the pig that won George's heart |url=http://www.dailymail.co.uk/tvshowbiz/article-420499/Grunt-peace-pig-won-Georges-heart.html |work=The Daily Mail |location=UK |date=December 4, 2006 |accessdate=January 4, 2009 }}</ref> She was briefly engaged to [[Charlie Sheen]] in 1990,<ref name="yahoo" /><ref name="girls">{{cite news |title=Charlie Sheen |first=Judy |last=Faber |url=http://www.cbsnews.com/stories/2006/08/24/entainment/main1931661.shtml |publisher=[[CBS]]	Preston married actor [[Kevin Gage (actor)|Kevin Gage]] in 1985 until their divorce in 1987.<ref> [http://articles.chicagotribune.com/2005-07-30/entertainment/0507300256_1_kelly-preston-celebrity-psychiatric-drugs "For Kelly Preston, life is more than 'Sky High'"], "[[Chicago Tribune]]", July 2005 </ref> Their only child, born during their marriage, is disabled. {{Citation needed|date=May 2012}} However, Preston refuses to acknowledge the child's existence in public, due to her beliefs as a scientologist. {{Citation needed|date=May 2012}} She also had a relationship with [[George Clooney]],<ref name="yahoo" /> who gave her [[Max (pig)|Max]], a pet pig that he kept after the couple split up.<ref>{{cite news |title=Grunt in peace, the pig that won George's heart |url=http://www.dailymail.co.uk/tvshowbiz/article-420499/Grunt-peace-pig-won-Georges-heart.html |work=The Daily Mail |location=UK |date=December 4, 2006 |accessdate=January 4, 2009 }}</ref> She w

Kelly Preston: Unscripted

|accessdate=October 30, 2009 | date=August 24, 2006}}</ref> but ended the relationship shortly after he accidentally shot her in the arm.<ref name="girls"/><ref> [http://www.thebiographychannel.co.uk/biographies/charlie-sheen.html "Charlie Sheen Biography"], [[Biography Channel]] website. Retrieved 26 October 2010.</ref>

briefly engaged to [[Charlie Sheen]] in 1990,<ref name="yahoo" /><ref name="girls">{{cite news |title=Charlie Sheen |first=Judy |last=Faber |url=http://www.cbsnews.com/stories/2006/08/24/entertainment/main1931661.shtml |publisher=[[CBS]] |accessdate=October 30, 2009 | date=August 24, 2006}}</ref> but ended the relationship shortly after he accidentally shot her in the arm.<ref name="girls"/><ref> [http://www.thebiographychannel.co.uk/biographies/charlie-sheen.html "Charlie Sheen Biography"], [[Biography Channel]] website. Retrieved 26 October 2010.</ref>

===== John Travolta =====

===== John Travolta =====

Revision as of 01:58, 23 May 2012

Kelly Preston (born October 13, 1962) is an American actress and former model.

Kelly Preston

Preston talking with Navy family members at the USO holiday party at Rockwell Hall Gym on Naval Amphibious Base Little Creek, Virginia, December 3, 2005.

Contents

- 1 Early years
- 2 Career
- 3 Personal life
    - 3.1 John Travolta
- 4 Filmography
- 5 References
- 6 External links

Early years

Preston was born **Kelly Kamalelehua Smith**[1] in Honolulu, Hawaii. Her mother, Linda,[2] was an administrator of a mental health center, and her father, who worked for an agricultural firm, drowned when Preston was three years old. [3] Her mother married Peter Palzis, a personnel director, who subsequently adopted her; she used his name when she first began her acting career until 1984.[1][4] She has a younger maternal half-brother, Chris Palzis.[1] As a child, she spent time living in Iraq and Australia. While living in Australia, she attended Pembroke School in Adelaide, South Australia. She later attended Punahou School and studied drama and theater at the University of Southern California.[5]

Kelly Preston: Unscripted

Career

While living in Australia, Preston was discovered at 16 by a fashion photographer who helped her get work in commercials and other small parts,[1] and organised Preston's first film audition in 1980 for the role of Emmeline in The Blue Lagoon (1980), which she lost to Brooke Shields.[6] At that time she changed her last name to Preston.[7] Her first prominent film roles came in 1985 romantic comedy teen flicks as Marilyn McCauley in *Mischief* and then Deborah Ann Fimple in *Secret Admirer*. Other notable roles included *SpaceCamp* (1986), *Twins* (1988) with Arnold Schwarzenegger and Danny DeVito, Avery Bishop in *Jerry Maguire* (1996) with Tom Cruise and Kate Newell in *Holy Man* (1998) with Eddie Murphy.

She played the girlfriend of her husband, John Travolta's, character "Terl" in the 2000 film *Battlefield Earth*,[8] and received "Worst Supporting Actress" at the 21st Golden Raspberry Awards for her role in the film.[9] In 2005 she appeared as the flying, superheroine mother of the protagonist in the film *Sky High*.

Born	Kelly Kamalelehua Smith October 13, 1962 Honolulu, Hawaii, U.S.
Occupation	model, actress
Years active	1980–present
Spouse	Kevin Gage (1986–1988, divorced) John Travolta (m. 1991–present)
Children	Preston's first child she had with her first husband Kevin Gage the child is disabled. Preston has three children with Travolta (1992–2009) Ella Bleu Travolta (b. 2000) Benjamin Hunter Kaleo Travolta (b. 2010)
Website	http://www.kellypreston.com/

Preston was featured in the chart-topping Maroon 5 music video, "She Will Be Loved" in 2004. The video features a love triangle and romantic scenes between Preston and Maroon 5 frontman Adam Levine. In 2008, she was cast in a television pilot for a potential show called *Suburban Shootout*.[10] She had a short term recurring role on *Medium*.[10]

In 2008, Preston starred in the Lifetime movie *The Tenth Circle*, directed by Peter Markle. The film was shot in Nova Scotia and featured Ron Eldard, Brittany Robertson, Michael Riley, Jamie Johnston and Geordie Brown. [11]

She is a spokeswoman for Neutrogena since 2005 and appears in print and television advertisements.[12]

Preston is set to play Victoria Gotti in the upcoming John Gotti biopic *Gotti: In The Shadow of my Father*. [citation needed]

Personal life

Preston married actor Kevin Gage in 1985 until their divorce in 1987.[13] Their only child, born during their marriage, is disabled.[citation needed] However, Preston refuses to acknowledge the child's existence in public, due to her beliefs as a scientologist.[citation needed] She also had a relationship with George Clooney,[1] who gave her Max, a pet pig that he kept after the couple split up.[14] She was briefly engaged to Charlie Sheen in 1990,[1][15] but ended the relationship shortly after he accidentally shot her in the arm.[15][16]

John Travolta

Kelly Preston: Unscripted

Preston first met John Travolta in 1987 while filming *The Experts*.[17] They married in 1991. Both traveled to Paris on an Air-France Concorde for a wedding ceremony at the Hotel de Crillon (close to the Place de la Concorde), celebrated on September 5, 1991. However, a second ceremony had to be conducted because the first, performed by a French Scientology minister (both Preston and Travolta are Scientologists), was regarded as invalid. The second ceremony took place a week later, on September 12, in Daytona Beach, Florida.[18] They have since had three children: Jett (April 13, 1992 - January, 2, 2009), Ella Bleu (born April 3, 2000) and Benjamin Hunter Kaleo (born November 23, 2010).

On January 2, 2009, their son Jett died while the family was on a holiday vacation in The Bahamas.[19][20] The cause of his death was attributed to a seizure.[21] Jett reportedly suffered from Kawasaki disease as an infant and had a history of seizures.[22][23] On September 24, 2009, [24] Travolta and Preston confirmed longstanding speculations when they testified that their son had autism and suffered regular seizures. This revelation came during their testimony at the trial resulting from an extortion attempt related to their son's death.[25]

On January 23, 2009, three people were arrested in the Bahamas in connection with a multi-million dollar extortion plot against Travolta and Preston around the circumstances of their son's death.[26] One of the men, Obie Wilchcombe, a member of the Bahamian Parliament and former Bahamian Minister of Tourism, was described as a "close friend" of Travolta and Preston.[26] Two others allegedly involved were an EMT named Tarino Lightbourne and a Bahamian senator named Pleasant Bridgewater. Bridgewater was charged with abetment to extort and conspiracy to extort and resigned from the Senate as a result of the allegations.[26][27]

In May 2010 Travolta and Preston announced that she was pregnant with the couple's third child.[28] At age 48 Preston delivered a healthy son, Benjamin Hunter Kaleo, on November 23, 2010.[29][30]

Marriage Agreement*

August 10, 1991

The undersigned agree to the following terms upon entering into this legal and binding marital partnership:

1) Kelly Preston shall receive a deed granting individual ownership of a dwelling of her choosing, valued at no less than $1,000,000 (one million dollars). All upkeep and expenses of the property, including but not limited to, maintenance and taxes, shall be paid by John Travolta and/or his corporations, which include: Alto, Inc., a Delaware corporation; Constellation Productions Inc., a California corporation; and Constellation Productions Inc., a Florida corporation. The residence, once chosen by Ms. Preston, will go into escrow immediately and close escrow in the name of Kelly Kamalelehua Preston. Ms. Preston shall hold all rights to the property.

2) Kelly Preston shall receive a three motion picture deal, as previously outlined during her private conference with studio representatives. The first picture shall begin production once Ms. Preston has selected a role and film from available properties. The three picture fulfillment deal is not to exceed a time period of more than two years from the date this agreement is signed. Any future films and/or productions offered to Ms. Preston, shall first be authorized and approved by John Travolta and/or his corporations previously listed, based exclusively on the profitability of the three guaranteed aforementioned films and roles.

3) Kelly Preston shall receive the sum of $500,000 (five hundred thousand dollars) for each full year of marriage to John Travolta. In addition, upon the birth of a/each child, Ms. Preston shall receive the sum of $50,000 (fifty thousand dollars). NOTE: In the event that any child is born with a birth defect or any condition which is deemed contrary to the accepted standards of the Church of Scientology, or should any defect or condition be discovered/diagnosed, prior to the child reaching legal adult age, Ms. Preston agrees to return all monies granted for the birth, in full, upon discovery/diagnosis.

4) A marriage ceremony between Kelly Preston and John Travolta shall take place in Paris, France, as chosen by Ms. Preston. The wedding party shall travel, all expenses paid, first class, by Concord jet, for said ceremony. Any and all costs incurred for the event, including but not limited to, venue, catering, entertainment, and security, shall be paid, in full, by John Travolta.

Signed under seal on this 10th day of August, 1991.

John Joseph Travolta

Kelly Kamalelehua Preston

*(This marriage agreement is a recreation of the document shown to me by my source, Anita.)

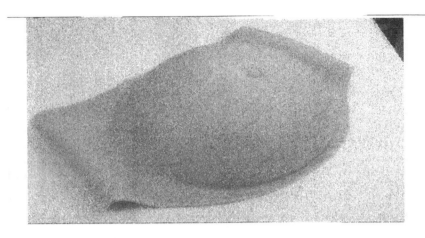

This photo shows a similar prosthetic to the one Preston allegedly wore to fake her pregnancy. When I saw the original, although identical, it was carefully wrapped in plastic. Preston's former personal assistant, Lu, said "this was to preserve Kelly's DNA in case I should ever need it."

Kelly Preston: Unscripted

Year	Title	Role	Notes
1980	*Hawaii Five-O*	Wendy	Episode: "For Old Times Sake"
1982	*Capitol*	Gillian McCandless	TV series
	Quincy M.E.	Ginger Reeves	Episode: "On Dying High"
	10 to Midnight	Doreen	
	CHiPs	Anna	Episode: "Things That Go Creep in the Night"
1983	*Metalstorm: The Destruction of Jared-Syn*	Dhyana	
	Christine	Roseanne	
	Lone Star	Redhead	TV movies
	For Love and Honor	Mary Lee	1983–1984 (12 episodes)
1984	*Riptide*	Sherry Meyers	Episode: "The Hardcase"
	Blue Thunder	Amy Braddock	Episode: "The Long Flight"
	Mischief	Marilyn McCauley	
1985	*Secret Admirer*	Deborah Anne Fimple	
1986	*SpaceCamp*	Tish Ambrosei	
	52 Pick-Up	Cini	
	Love at Stake	Sara Lee	
1987	*A Tiger's Tale*	Shirley Butts	
	Amazon Women on the Moon	Violet	Segment, "Titan Man"
	Twins	Marnie Mason	
1988	*The Experts*	Bonnie	
	Spellbinder	Miranda Reed	
1990	*Tales from the Crypt*	Linda	Episode: "The Switch"
1991	*Run*	Karen Landers	
	The Perfect Bride	Laura	TV movie
1992	*Only You*	Amanda Hughes	
1993	*The American Clock*	Diana Marley	TV movie
	Love Is a Gun	Jean Starr	
1994	*Double Cross*	Vera Blanchard	
	Cheyenne Warrior	Rebecca Carver	TV movies
	Little Surprises	Ginger	
1995	*Mrs. Munck*	Young Rose	
	Citizen Ruth	Rachel	
1996	*From Dusk till Dawn*	Kelly Hogue	

Year	Title	Role	Notes
	Curdled		
	Jerry Maguire	Avery Bishop	
1997	*Addicted to Love*	Linda	
	Nothing to Lose	Ann Beam	
1998	*Holy Man*	Kate Newell	
	Jack Frost	Gabby Frost	
1999	*For Love of the Game*	Jane Aubrey	
	Bar Hopping	Bebe	TV movie
2000	*Battlefield Earth*	Chirk	Razzie Award for Worst Supporting Actress
2001	*Daddy and Them*	Rose	
2002	*Fear Factor*	Herself	
	View from the Top	Sherry	
2003	*What a Girl Wants*	Libby Reynolds	
	The Cat in the Hat	Joan Walden	Nominated—Razzie Award for Worst Supporting Actress
	Eulogy	Lucy Collins	
2004	*Return to Sender*	Susan Kennan	
	Joey	Donna Di Gregorio	Episodes: "Joey and the Dream Girl: Parts 1 and 2"
	Fat Actress	Quinn Taylor Scott	4 episodes
2005	*Sky High*	Josie Stronghold / Jetstream	
2006	*Broken Bridges*	Angela Dalton	
2007	*Death Sentence*	Helen Hume	
	Struck	Trista	
2008	*Medium*	Meghan Doyle	4 episodes
	The Tenth Circle	Laura Stone	TV movie
	Suburban Shootout	Camilla Diamond	TV series
2009	*Old Dogs*	Vicki	
	Casino Jack	Pam Abramoff	
2010	*The Last Song*	Kim	
	From Paris with Love	Woman on Eiffel tower	uncredited cameo
2013	*Gotti: In The Shadow of my Father*	Victoria "Vicki" Gotti	post-production

Kelly Preston: Unscripted

References

1. ^ *a b c d e f* "Kelly Preston Biography" (http://movies.yahoo.com/movie/contributor/1800016652/bio) . *movies.yahoo.com.* Yahoo! Movies. http://movies.yahoo.com/movie/contributor/1800016652/bio. Retrieved August 22, 2010.
2. ^ Donnelly, Dave. "Hawaii." (http://archives.starbulletin.com/1999/05/17/features/donnelly.html) *Honolulu Star-Bulletin.* May 17, 1999.
3. ^ "Kelly Preston Profile" (http://uk.eonline.com/uberblog/celebs/c113179_kelly_preston.html) . *uk.eonline.com.* E! Online. http://uk.eonline.com/uberblog/celebs/c113179_kelly_preston.html. Retrieved August 22, 2010.
4. ^ "Kelly Preston Biography (1962–)" (http://www.filmreference.com/film/45/Kelly-Preston.html) . *FilmReference.com.* NetIndustries, LLC. http://www.filmreference.com/film/45/Kelly-Preston.html. Retrieved August 22, 2010.
5. ^ "About Kelly" (http://www.kellypreston.com/) . Kelly Preston.com. http://www.kellypreston.com/. Retrieved February 26, 2008.
6. ^ IMDB Biography of Kelly Preston (http://www.imdb.com/name/nm0000593/bio)
7. ^ Kelly Preston Vitals (http://www.askmen.com/celebs/women/actress/38_kelly_preston.html) at Ask Men.com
8. ^ Graham, Bob (January 19, 2001). "Travolta's Demolition Derby; Comic-book nuttiness lifts 'Battlefield Earth'" (http://www.sfgate.com/cgi-bin/article.cgi?f=/c/a/2001/01/19/DD162654.DTL) . *San Francisco Chronicle* (Hearst Communications). http://www.sfgate.com/cgi-bin/article.cgi?f=/c/a/2001/01/19/DD162654.DTL. Retrieved June 12, 2008.
9. ^ Grant, John (2006). *Sci-Fi Movies: Facts, Figures & Fun.* Sterling Publishing Company. pp. 87. ISBN 1-904332-35-8.
10. ^ *a b* Trechak, Brad (May 16, 2008). "Kelly Preston in new HBO series" (http://www.tvsquad.com/2008/05/16/kelly-preston-in-new-hbo-series/) . *TV Squad.* http://www.tvsquad.com/2008/05/16/kelly-preston-in-new-hbo-series/. Retrieved June 12, 2008.
11. ^ "The Tenth Circle" (http://www.imdb.com/title/tt1132288/) . IMDB. http://www.imdb.com/title/tt1132288/. Retrieved Jul 4, 2010.
12. ^ "Kelly Preston Fronts Neutrogena" (http://www.monstersandcritics.com/people/news/article_3702.php/Kelly_Preston_Fronts_Neutrogena) January 20, 2005, Monsters and Critics
13. ^ "For Kelly Preston, life is more than 'Sky High'" (http://articles.chicagotribune.com/2005-07-30/entertainment/0507300256_1_kelly-preston-celebrity-psychiatric-drugs) , *Chicago Tribune,* July 30, 2005
14. ^ "Grunt in peace, the pig that won George's heart" (http://www.dailymail.co.uk/tvshowbiz/article-420499/Grunt-peace-pig-won-Georges-heart.html) . *The Daily Mail* (UK). December 4, 2006. http://www.dailymail.co.uk/tvshowbiz/article-420499/Grunt-peace-pig-won-Georges-heart.html. Retrieved January 4, 2009.
15. ^ *a b* Faber, Judy (August 24, 2006). "Charlie Sheen" (http://www.cbsnews.com/stories/2006/08/24/entertainment/main1931661.shtml) . CBS. http://www.cbsnews.com/stories/2006/08/24/entertainment/main1931661.shtml. Retrieved October 30, 2009.
16. ^ "Charlie Sheen Biography" (http://www.thebiographychannel.co.uk/biographies/charlie-sheen.html) . Biography Channel website. Retrieved 26 October 2010.
17. ^ Bob and Sheri Stritof. "Kelly Preston and John Travolta Marriage Profile." (http://marriage.about.com/od/entertainment1/a/johntravolta.htm) about.com. Retrieved January 4, 2009.
18. ^ "John Travolta Biography" (http://www.enewsreference.com/actors/john_travolta.html) . Enewsreference.com. http://www.enewsreference.com/actors/john_travolta.html. Retrieved August 4, 2009.
19. ^ "Jett Travolta, son of actors, dies at 16" (http://www.cnn.com/2009/SHOWBIZ/Movies/01/02/obit.jett.travolta/) . CNN. January 2, 2009. http://www.cnn.com/2009/SHOWBIZ/Movies/01/02/obit.jett.travolta/. Retrieved January 2, 2009.
20. ^ "John Travolta's teenage son dies" (http://news.bbc.co.uk/2/hi/entertainment/7809172.stm) . *BBC News* (BBC). January 2, 2009. http://news.bbc.co.uk/2/hi/entertainment/7809172.stm. Retrieved January 2, 2009.
21. ^ "Death Certificate: John Travolta's Son Died of a Seizure" (http://abcnews.go.com/Entertainment/MindMoodNews/story?id=6576215&page=1) . ABC News. January 5, 2009. http://abcnews.go.com/Entertainment/MindMoodNews/story?id=6576215&page=1. Retrieved January 5, 2009.
22. ^ "John Travolta's 16-Year-Old Son Dies" (http://www.people.com/people/article/0,,20249865,00.html) . *People,* January 2, 2009. http://www.people.com/people/article/0,,20249865,00.html. Retrieved January 4, 2009.

Kelly Preston: Unscripted

23. ^ Errico, Marcus (January 2, 2009). "John Travolta's Son Jett Dead at 16" (http://uk.eonline.com/uberblog/b77259_john_travoltas_son_jett_dead_16.html) . E! Online. http://uk.eonline.com/uberblog/b77259_john_travoltas_son_jett_dead_16.html. Retrieved January 2, 2009.
24. ^ Heureux, Steve L. (September 24, 2009). "Travolta finally admits that son had Autism" (http://www.examiner.com/x-17410-Toledo-Autism--Parenting-Examiner~y2009m9d24-Travolta-finally-admits-that-son-had-Autism) . The Examiner. http://www.examiner.com/x-17410-Toledo-Autism--Parenting-Examiner~y2009m9d24-Travolta-finally-admits-that-son-had-Autism. Retrieved September 24, 2009.
25. ^ Abraham, Mary Rose (September 23, 2009). "From John Travolta: I Ran Down the Stairs To Help My Son" (http://abcnews.go.com/Entertainment/john-travolta-bahamas-testify-extortion-case/story?id=8649816) . ABC News. http://abcnews.go.com/Entertainment/john-travolta-bahamas-testify-extortion-case/story?id=8649816. Retrieved September 23, 2009.
26. ^ a b c Harlow, John (January 25, 2009). "Senator 'tried to extort cash' from Travolta over son's death" (http://www.timesonline.co.uk/tol/news/world/us_and_americas/article5581456.ece) . The Sunday Times (UK). http://www.timesonline.co.uk/tol/news/world/us_and_americas/article5581456.ece. Retrieved January 25, 2009.
27. ^ "Travolta Suspect Resigns" (http://www.tmz.com/2009/01/24/travolta-suspect-resigns/) . TMZ.com. January 24, 2009. http://www.tmz.com/2009/01/24/travolta-suspect-resigns/. Retrieved January 25, 2009.
28. ^ "John Travolta and Kelly Preston Are Expecting!" (http://www.people.com/people/article/0,,20386272,00.html) . People. May 18, 2010. http://www.people.com/people/article/0,,20386272,00.html. Retrieved May 18, 2010.
29. ^ "John Travolta and Kelly Preston Welcome Son Benjamin" (http://celebritybabies.people.com/2010/11/24/john-travolta-kelly-preston-welcome-son-benjamin/) . People. November 24, 2010. http://celebritybabies.people.com/2010/11/24/john-travolta-kelly-preston-welcome-son-benjamin/. Retrieved November 24, 2010.
30. ^ "Kelly Preston's Post-Baby Body Secret? Breastfeeding" (http://celebritybabies.people.com/2011/04/13/kelly-prestons-post-baby-body-secret-breastfeeding/) April 13, 2011, People

External links

- Official website (http://www.kellypreston.com/)
- Kelly Preston (http://www.imdb.com/name/nm0000593/) at the Internet Movie Database
- Kelly Preston (http://www.allrovi.com/name/p57732) at AllRovi
- Healthy Child Healthy World (http://healthychild.org/)
- Kelly Preston in Denmark interview (Danish and English) (http://www.overgaard.dk/kelly_preston.html)

Retrieved from "http://en.wikipedia.org/w/index.php?title=Kelly_Preston&oldid=493922362"

Categories: 1962 births | Living people | 20th-century actors | 21st-century actors | Actors from Hawaii | American adoptees | American expatriates in Australia | American female models | American film actors | American Scientologists | American shooting survivors | American television actors | People educated at Pembroke School, Adelaide | People from Honolulu, Hawaii | Punahou School alumni | University of Southern California alumni

- This version of the page has been revised.
  Besides normal editing, the reason for revision may have been that this version contains factual inaccuracies, vandalism, or material not compatible with the Creative Commons Attribution-ShareAlike License.

Kelly Preston

From Wikipedia, the free encyclopedia

This is an old revision of this page, as edited by 68.207.145.46 (talk) at 17:21, 11 December 2005. The present address (URL) is a permanent link to this revision, which may differ significantly from the current revision (https://en.wikipedia.org/wiki/Kelly_Preston).

(diff) ← Previous revision | Latest revision (diff) | Newer revision → (diff)

Kelly Kamalelehua Palzis (born October 13, 1962 in Honolulu, Hawaii) is an American actress.

File:Kelly Preston2.jpg
Kelly Preston

Contents

* 1 Modeling
* 2 Marriage
* 3 Trivia
* 4 Partial Filmography
* 5 External links

Modeling

Preston had a modeling career when she was a teenager. At 16, she was discovered by a fashion photographer who helped her get acting work in commercials and other small parts, which eventually developed into a successful movie career.

Marriage

Preston has been married to John Travolta since 1991. Preston put her career on hold after the wedding, opting to be a wife and mother when Travolta's career took off again in the 1990s. The couple have two children, a son and a daughter; she also has a son by her first marriage to actor Kevin Gage. Kelly does not use the surname "Travolta" professionally.

Both Preston and Travolta are Scientologists, and Preston appeared in the film *Battlefield Earth* (produced by John Travolta, based on the novel by Scientology founder L. Ron Hubbard). Her role is sometimes incorrectly described as "starring" even though she only appears in one scene. She plays a Psychlo female encountered in a bar (possibly a prostitute) whose primary talent is implied to be fellatio.

Recently, she has taken up the issue of overmedication and children. In keeping with Scientology precepts, Preston believes that schools are forcing or pressuring students and their families to medicate them for ADD unnecessarily. She has testified before the Florida state legislature encouraging the passage of a bill to ban such practice. While there is already a federal law to that effect, only schools receiving federal funding are subject to its terms.

She also devotes much of her time as a board member of the Children's Health Environmental Coalition (http://www.checnet.org/) (CHEC), a non-profit organization dedicated to educating parents about environmental toxins and potential health hazards for children with illnesses. She joined after their son Jett was diagnosed with Kawasaki syndrome, an illness that mostly affects children and results in severe allergies and asthma attacks.

Trivia

- Preston's former boyfriends include George Clooney and Charlie Sheen. After living with Sheen for one year (and receiving a very large diamond ring from him), Preston ended the relationship in 1990 shortly after an incident in which Sheen accidentally shot her in the arm.

- John Travolta married Kelly Preston twice. Their first wedding (September 5, 1991) was performed by a French Scientologist minister, but it was later declared illegal. They married again within the month.

- In 2004, Kelly Preston was featured in the chart-topping Maroon 5 music video, "She Will Be Loved". The video features a dangerous love triangle and some steamy romantic scenes between Preston and Maroon 5 frontman Adam Levine.

Partial Filmography

- *Sky High* (2005)
- *Eulogy* (2004)
- *The Cat in the Hat* (2003)
- *What a Girl Wants* (2003)
- *View from the Top* (2003)
- *Battlefield Earth* (2000)
- *Addicted to Love* (1997)
- *Jerry Maguire* (1996)
- *Curdled* (1996)
- *From Dusk Till Dawn* (1996)
- *Citizen Ruth* (1996)
- *Waiting to Exhale* (1995) (uncredited)
- *Only You* (1992)
- *Twins* (1988)
- *Amazon Women on the Moon* (1987)
- *SpaceCamp* (1986)
- *Secret Admirer* (1985)
- *Christine* (1983)
- *Capitol* (1982) (TV series)

External links

- Kelly Preston (http://www.imdb.com/name/nm0000593/) at the Internet Movie Database

216

Kelly Preston: Unscripted

Categories: 1962 births | Honolulans | American actors | Film actors | Scientologists | Worst Supporting Actress Razzie

- This version of the page has been revised. Besides normal editing, the reason for revision may have been that this version contains factual inaccuracies, vandalism, or material not compatible with the Creative Commons Attribution-ShareAlike License.

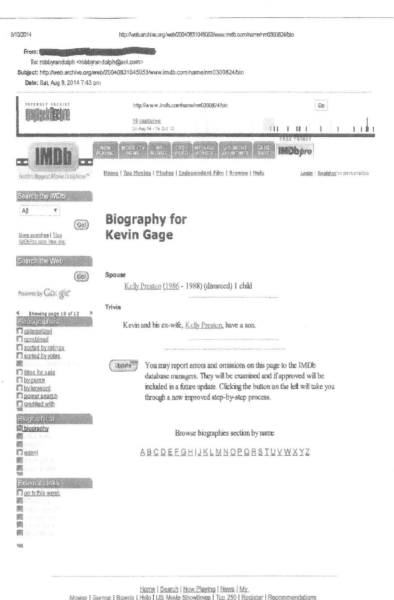

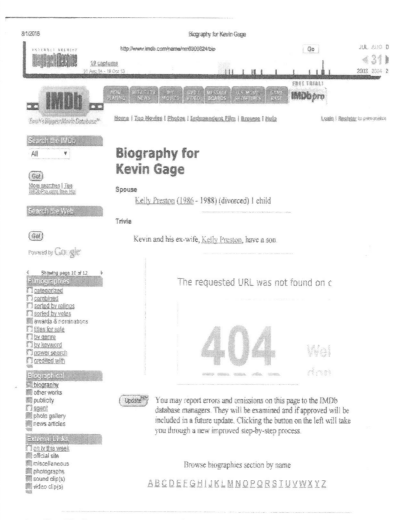

http://www.imdb.com/name/nm0000824/bio   Go   JUL AUG D

19 captures   ◀ 31 ▶
31 Aug 04 - 19 Oct 13   2003 2004 2

Home | Top Movies | Photos | Independent Film | Browse | Help   Login | Register to personalize

Biography for
Kevin Gage

Spouse

    Kelly Preston (1986 - 1988) (divorced) 1 child

Trivia

    Kevin and his ex-wife, Kelly Preston, have a son.

The requested URL was not found on c

404   Wel
                 don

(Update)   You may report errors and omissions on this page to the IMDb database managers. They will be examined and if approved will be included in a future update. Clicking the button on the left will take you through a new improved step-by-step process.

Browse biographies section by name

A B C D E F G H I J K L M N O P Q R S T U V W X Y Z

Home | Search | Now Playing | News | My Movies | Games | Boards | Help | US Movie Showtimes | Top 250 | Register | Recommendations | Box Office | Index | Trailers | IMDbPro.com - Free Trial | IMDb Publicity Photos

The Truth About
Scientology

Google™

Google Search
    WWW
⦿ truthaboutscientology.com

Altering the Tech
Sources for Standard Tech

Scientology's Statistics
Got M/Us?
Knowledge Reports
CoS Outpoints
Erasing History
Things to Think About

Send Me Stuff!

This site relies on official
Scientology publications. If you
have magazines or mailings you
can share, please contact me.

Recommended Reading
Scientology's DMCA Complaint
Legal Threat from Scientology
Protecting Your Privacy
Determining What's True

Site created by Kristi Wachter,
creator of Scientology Lies

this site discusses the Church of
Scientology but is not affiliated
with them in any way. You can
find their official site at
www.scientology.org

Kelly Preston - Scientology Service Completions

TAS : Scientology Statistics : Individual Completions : K : Kelly Preston

A B C D E F G H I J K L M N O P Q R S T U V W X Y Z

Note: Preliminary analysis suggests that about 60% of people who try
Scientology do only a single course or service, that 80% of new members
become inactive within 2 years, and that 65% of those who reach the level
of Clear become inactive within a year after doing so. The older a list, the
more likely that a person listed on it is no longer involved in Scientology.
Please read About These Lists for more information.

Kelly Preston in Scientology's Published Service Completion Lists

The following 27 individual completions for Kelly Preston appear in official
Scientology publications:

Kelly Preston	PURIFICATION RUNDOWN	Celebrity 222	1988-10-01
Kelly Preston	HOW TO IMPROVE RELATIONSHIPS WITH OTHERS COURSE	Celebrity 242	1990-11-01
Kelly Preston	SUCCESS THROUGH COMMUNICATION COURSE	Celebrity 242	1990-11-01
Kelly Preston	ARC STRAIGHTWIRE	Source 73	1990-11-01
Kelly Preston	PERSONAL VALUES AND INTEGRITY	Celebrity 244	1991-02-01
Kelly Preston	HOW TO IMPROVE RELATIONSHIPS WITH OTHERS	Celebrity 244	1991-02-01
Kelly Preston	STARTING A SUCCESSFUL MARRIAGE	Celebrity 244	1991-02-01
Kelly Preston	SUCCESS THROUGH COMMUNICATION COURSE	Celebrity 244	1991-02-01
Kelly Preston	CLEAR	Celebrity 244	1991-02-01
Kelly Preston	CLEAR	Celebrity 248	1991-10-01
Kelly Preston	GRADE II	Celebrity 248	1991-10-01
Kelly Preston	L 11 NEW LIFE RUNDOWN	Source 78	1991-12-01
Kelly Preston	GRADE II	Celebrity 250	1992-01-01
Kelly Preston	STUDENT HAT COURSE	Celebrity 252	1992-03-01
Kelly Preston	L 12 FLAG OT EXECUTIVE RUNDOWN	Source 79	1992-03-01

Kelly Preston	FALSE PURPOSE RUNDOWN LISTS	Celebrity 272	1993-12-01
Kelly Preston	ELIGIBILITY FOR ISSUE OF OT LEVELS CHECK	Source 92	1994-05-01
Kelly Preston	OT II	Source 93	1994-08-01
Kelly Preston	OT III	Advance 122	1994-12-01
Kelly Preston	NEW OT IV	Advance 122	1994-12-01
Kelly Preston	LIFE ORIENTATION COURSE	Celebrity 283	1995-05-01
Kelly Preston	L 10	Source 100	1996-04-01
Kelly Preston	NEW OT V AUDITED NOTS	Source 101	1996-07-01
Kelly Preston	NEW OT V AUDITED NOTS	Source 102	1996-09-01
Kelly Preston	STUDY CERTAINTY COURSE	Celebrity 331	2001-05-01
Kelly Preston	NEW OT VI HUBBARD SOLO NOTS AUDITING COURSE	Source 137	2002-02-01
Kelly Preston	PTS/SP Course	Celebrity 351	2003-09-01

Note: The dates listed above are the approximate publication dates of the magazines, which may be weeks or months later than the actual date the service was completed.

Kelly Preston in Scientology's Publications

The following 1 mentions of Kelly Preston appear in official Scientology publications:

Kelly Preston	Members with Honor Status	Impact 114	2006-09-01

Note: The dates listed above are the approximate publication dates of the magazines, which may be weeks or months later than the actual date the service was completed.

Kelly Preston and the Clear List

No entries were found in my Scientology Statistics Project Clear List database for this person.

Kelly Preston and Scientologist Online Sites

My database does not list a Scientologist Online cookie-cutter web site for this person.

221

The Truth About Scientology

Google™

Google Search
- www
- * truthaboutscientology.com

Aking the Tech
Sources for Standard Tech

Scientology's Statistics
Got M/Us?
Knowledge Reports
CoS Outpoints
Erasing History
Things to Think About

Send Me Stuff!

This site relies on official Scientology publications. If you have magazines or mailings you can share, please contact me.

Recommended Reading
Scientology's DMCA Complaint
Legal Threat from Scientology
Protecting Your Privacy
Determining What's True

Site created by Kristi Wachter, creator of Scientology Lies

this site discusses the Church of Scientology but is not affiliated with them in any way. You can find their official site at www.scientology.org

Linda Carlson - Scientology Service Completions

TAS : Scientology Statistics : Individual Completions : L : Linda Carlson

A B C D E F G H I J K L M N O P Q R S T U V W X Y Z

Note: Preliminary analysis suggests that about 60% of people who try Scientology do only a single course or service, that 80% of new members become inactive within 2 years, and that 65% of those who reach the level of Clear become inactive within a year after doing so. The older a list, the more likely that a person listed on it is no longer involved in Scientology. Please read About These Lists for more information.

Linda Carlson in Scientology's Published Service Completion Lists

The following 28 individual completions for Linda Carlson appear in official Scientology publications:

Linda Carlson	SUNSHINE RUNDOWN	Source 58	1987-07-01
Linda Carlson	OT DEBUG SERVICE	Freewinds 16	1995-06-01
Linda Carlson	OT DEBUG SERVICE	Freewinds 19	1996-04-01
Linda Carlson	PURIFICATION RUNDOWN	Source 102	1996-09-01
Linda Carlson	POWER PROCESSING	Auditor 301	2002-07-01
Linda Carlson	POWER PLUS PROCESSING	Auditor 301	2002-07-01
Linda Carlson	OT PREPARATIONS	Auditor 301	2002-07-01
Linda Carlson	SOLO COURSE PART I	Advance 168	2003-10-01
Linda Carlson	OT ELIGIBILITY	Advance 168	2003-10-01
Linda Carlson	R6EW	Advance 169	2003-11-01
Linda Carlson	NED CASE COMPLETION	Advance 171	2004-03-01
Linda Carlson	SUNSHINE RUNDOWN AUDITING	Advance 171	2004-03-01
Linda Carlson	THE CLEARING COURSE	Advance 171	2004-03-01
Linda Carlson	OT I	Advance 171	2004-03-01
Linda Carlson	NED CASE COMPLETION	Source 153	2004-04-01

Linda Carlson - Scientology Service Completions | Truth About Scientology Statistics Project

Linda Carlson	SUNSHINE RUNDOWN AUDITING	Source 153	2004-04-01
Linda Carlson	THE CLEARING COURSE	Source 153	2004-04-01
Linda Carlson	OT I	Source 153	2004-04-01
Linda Carlson	OT II	Source 154	2004-04-01
Linda Carlson	OT III	Source 154	2004-04-01
Linda Carlson	OT II	Advance 172	2004-04-01
Linda Carlson	OT III	Advance 172	2004-04-01
Linda Carlson	OT IV	Source 155	2004-05-01
Linda Carlson	OT V	Source 155	2004-05-01
Linda Carlson	OT IV	Advance 173	2004-06-01
Linda Carlson	OT V	Advance 173	2004-06-01
Linda Carlson	PTS/SP Course	Source 167	2005-06-01
Linda Carlson	NEW OT VI HUBBARD SOLO NOTS AUDITING COURSE	Source 171	2005-10-01

Note: The dates listed above are the approximate publication dates of the magazines, which may be weeks or months later than the actual date the service was completed.

Linda Carlson in Scientology's Publications

The following 1 mentions of Linda Carlson appear in official Scientology publications:

Linda Carlson	Honor Roll	Impact 114	2006-09-01

Note: The dates listed above are the approximate publication dates of the magazines, which may be weeks or months later than the actual date the service was completed.

Linda Carlson and the Clear List

No entries were found in my Scientology Statistics Project Clear List database for this person.

- - -

Kelly Preston: Unscripted

The Truth About Scientology

Google™

Google Search
- WWW
- truthaboutscientology.com

Altering the Tech
Sources for Standard Tech

Scientology's Statistics
Got M/Us?
Knowledge Reports
CoS Outpoints
Erasing History
Things to Think About

Send Me Stuff!

This site relies on official Scientology publications. If you have magazines or mailings you can share, please contact me.

Recommended Reading
Scientology's DMCA Complaint
Legal Threat from Scientology
Protecting Your Privacy
Determining What's True

Site created by Kristi Wachter, creator of Scientology Lies

this site discusses the Church of Scientology but is not affiliated with them in any way. You can find their official site at www.scientology.org

Chris Palzis - Scientology Service Completions

TAS : Scientology Statistics : Individual Completions : C : Chris Palzis

A B C D E F G H I J K L M N O P Q R S T U V W X Y Z

Note: Preliminary analysis suggests that about 60% of people who try Scientology do only a single course or service, that 80% of new members become inactive within 2 years, and that 65% of those who reach the level of Clear become inactive within a year after doing so. The older a list, the more likely that a person listed on it is no longer involved in Scientology. Please read About These Lists for more information.

Chris Palzis in Scientology's Published Service Completion Lists

The following 1 individual completions for Chris Palzis appear in official Scientology publications:

| Chris Palzis | SUCCESS THROUGH COMMUNICATION COURSE | Celebrity 321 | 1999-10-01 |

Note: The dates listed above are the approximate publication dates of the magazines, which may be weeks or months later than the actual date the service was completed.

Chris Palzis in Scientology's Publications

No entries were found in my main Scientology Statistics database for this person.

Chris Palzis and the Clear List

No entries were found in my Scientology Statistics Project Clear List database for this person.

Chris Palzis and Scientologist Online Sites

My database does not list a Scientologist Online cookie-cutter web site for this person.

Chris Palzis and WISE Directories

WISE, the World Institute of Scientology Enterprises, publishes directories listing their members.

My database does not list this person in the most recent WISE directories.

The Truth About Scientology

Google™

Google Search

- WWW
- * truthaboutscientology.com

Altering the Tech

Sources for Standard Tech

Scientology's Statistics

Got M/Us?

Knowledge Reports

CoS Outpoints

Erasing History

Things to Think About

Send Me Stuff!

This site relies on official Scientology publications. If you have magazines or mailings you can share, please contact me.

Recommended Reading

Scientology's DMCA Complaint

Legal Threat from Scientology

Protecting Your Privacy

Determining What's True

Site created by Kristi Wachter, creator of Scientology Lies

this site discusses the Church of Scientology but is not affiliated with them in any way. You can find their official site at www.scientology.org

Peter Palzis - Scientology Service Completions

TAS : Scientology Statistics : Individual Completions : P : Peter Palzis

A B C D E F G H I J K L M N O P Q R S T U V W X Y Z

Note: Preliminary analysis suggests that about 60% of people who try Scientology do only a single course or service, that 80% of new members become inactive within 2 years, and that 65% of those who reach the level of Clear become inactive within a year after doing so. The older a list, the more likely that a person listed on it is no longer involved in Scientology. Please read About These Lists for more information.

Peter Palzis in Scientology's Published Service Completion Lists

The following 1 individual completions for Peter Palzis appear in official Scientology publications:

Peter Palzis	HOW TO IMPROVE RELATIONSHIPS WITH OTHERS	Celebrity 306	1997-09-01

Note: The dates listed above are the approximate publication dates of the magazines, which may be weeks or months later than the actual date the service was completed.

Peter Palzis in Scientology's Publications

No entries were found in my main Scientology Statistics database for this person.

Peter Palzis and the Clear List

No entries were found in my Scientology Statistics Project Clear List database for this person.

Peter Palzis and Scientologist Online Sites

My database does not list a Scientologist Online cookie-cutter web site for this person.

Peter Palzis and WISE Directories

WISE, the World Institute of Scientology Enterprises, publishes directories listing their members.

My database does not list this person in the most recent WISE directories.

The information on this page comes from my Scientology Statistics database. While I attempt to be as accurate as possible, errors or inaccuracies may be introduced by the source material, the transcription process, or database bugs. If you discover an error or problem, please let me know by writing to kristi@truthaboutscientology.com.

COMING SOON!

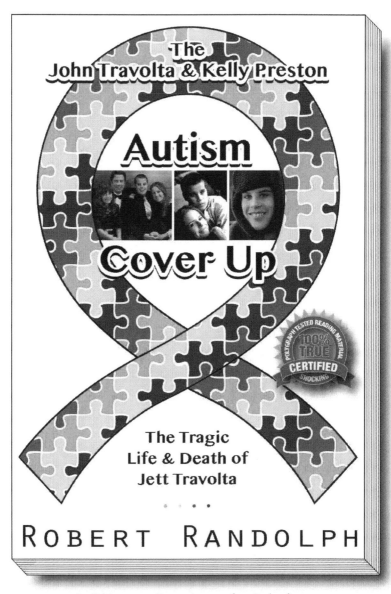

Available soon online and at your favorite book store.

WORLD EXCLUSIVE

PREVIEW

The John Travolta and Kelly Preston

Autism Cover Up!

"The stories would imply the death of my son was intentional, and I was culpable somehow"

John Travolta — (2009)

The John Travolta and Kelly Preston

Autism Cover Up!

INTRODUCTION

I believed I had written all I had to say regarding the tragic life and unnecessary death of Jett Travolta; how this unfortunate child was overlooked and neglected by his famous, wealthy parents. You can bet something is inherently wrong with the values and belief structure of the very people charged with protecting and raising an innocent child in today's "image is everything" world, when they Photoshop, from birth, that child to conceal his illness from the public.

I woke up the other day and turned on the news – a woman named Marcia Hinds was being interviewed; she has a son, Ryan, who was born with Autism. Through Ryan's family's unconditional love and devotion, they were able to change the quality and course of his life. He is currently living as an active, productive adult, with absolutely no signs of the often debilitating disease. I was moved, close to tears, with Marcia's story. It took me less than five minutes before I was online, purchasing her book, *I Know You're In There*. I read it in record time, absorbed in her gripping story.

As I read, my heart couldn't help but ache for Jett Travolta; how he was denied the simplest, most basic element in his life – LOVE. Due to his parent's following the Church of Scientology dogma, Jett was also denied the medical attention he so desperately needed. As I struggled to suppress the thoughts haunting me about Jett, and attempted to put them out of my head, it occurred to me that I was doing precisely what his own parents did . . . *ignoring the issue.*

All at once, I felt compelled to tell his *true story*, bluntly and to the point. As this revelation hit me, I went on about my day but could not get Jett out of my head. I was well aware of the way Travolta had been lying to the world about his homosexuality, after all, I had already written three books based on that very subject. Believe me when I tell you, I was more than done with this man. Or so I thought! I had written the three previous books to set the record straight and because so many victims of Travolta had reached out to me for help. It was truly a heavy burden I carried for these men, ever putting my own life in harm's way. I received death threats, which I believed originated from Travolta and his cohorts at the Church of

Scientology. These death threats had pretty much become a way of life for me since I had the audacity to speak up and expose Travolta's lies.

When moving forward with this book, my eyes were wide open to the possibility that same pattern of intimidation that would likely continue. Nevertheless, something deep within kept pushing me to follow through. I must do it. With the help of many inside sources, I would answer the questions Jett's untimely demise had posed.

Up to this point, the only information out there concerning Jett's life and death, was the smokescreen Travolta and Preston had presented to the world. The record should be set straight for the young man who was left to die – alone – on a bathroom floor, while in the Bahamas with his family. Meanwhile, his parents were partying with friends, toasting in the New Year.

The Travolta's came dangerously close to being exposed for what they had done to Jett. But as always, they, along with the CoS and their public relations team, put together a plan which proved to be quite effective. The conveniently timed announcement that they were expecting another child, was intended to show how life goes on. In reality, it was just another crock of shit to throw the public off the track from the suspicions and rumors of parental neglect.

Jett Travolta lived his short life under the rule of L. Ron Hubbard and the insanity of his preaching, at the same time failing to live up to his famous parent's expectations of having the "perfect child." The world will learn how this child is the product of a ridiculous, prearranged marriage between a homosexual and a selfish, drug and alcohol addicted woman. The only constant in Travolta and Preston's lives, from the beginning, has been the pretenses in the name of fame.

If not for the fact that I heard from so many verifiable sources, this book would not be possible. Those who reached out to me include: Immediate family members of both Travolta and Preston, close friends, associates, employees (past and present), neighbors from California, Florida, Hawaii and the Bahamas. All claiming to have a close and inside view at the truth to the Travolta/Preston *cover-up*.

I made a promise to myself that I will leave no stone unturned regarding these two hypocrites. With my own two eyes, I personally witnessed the child abuse which took place on

January 30, 2007. I watched, and actually have pictures, of Jett, as he was left unattended in a spa looking for his father. It was heart wrenching to watch the boy as he searched the facility, apparently lost and confused. Jeff Kathrein, Jett's then nanny as well as one of Travolta's lovers, was shoving pills down Jett's throat in an obvious effort to calm him down. This is the same man who reportedly discovered Jett's dead body in the bathroom after he had been left unsupervised for over ten hours. This man allegedly played a huge part in the cover-up and once I share with you the information his family and friends told me, you too, will agree that there was, in fact, a cover-up. Many shared their theories about the night in question while others shared facts, which only insiders and family could possibly know.

Jett's parents were free to pursue their own dreams and goals, so why did they feel it is okay to sweep their deceased son's life under the rug? That question will be addressed as the truth comes to light. My objective, in writing this book, was to bring awareness and hope for the parents of children with autism. Just as Marcia Hinds would write such a wonderful book, surely there are many other parents eager to alter the fate of their own children. Hopefully, this book will serve as a source of hope and information to the world, regarding this misunderstood disease.

When I decided to take this project on, I knew how important it was to get it just right. This was a much more significant topic than Travolta's lurid sex life. If I do get it right and spread awareness, millions of parents could have new found hope. Detailing Travolta and Preston's pathetic, and often criminal, attempts at parenting, will serve as a heart-wrenching example of what *not* to do. In sharp contrast, many wonderful instances of great parenting will be exemplified as well. An excellent example is Marcia Hinds and her story of her son Ryan.

I'm confident that by the time you are finished reading this true story, you will have a comprehensive awareness of what Jett Travolta must have endured during his short sixteen years of life. There was clearly child neglect and inexcusable abuse from his two famous parents.

"After reading this book and learning the facts that were presented to me . . . you can decide for yourself what really happened to Jett Travolta"

Robert Randolph — (2015)

Made in the USA
Lexington, KY
13 November 2015